ARCHITECTURAL ACADEMICIAN

M.Y. GINZBURG

ARCHITECTURE
OF THE NKTP
SANATORIUM
IN KISLOVODSK

MOSCOW • 1940

PARTICIPANTS
IN DESIGNING AND BUILDING THE SANATORIUM

Project leader and chief architect: *M.Y. Ginzburg*. Authors and participants in particular parts of the construction project: Block No. 1 — author arch. *S.Y. Vakhtangov* assisted by *T.B. Rappoport*; interior design — *I.I. Leonidov* and *L.S. Bogdanov*; structural engineer *N.D. Vishnevsky*. Block No. 2 — authors arch. *Y.M. Popov* and *Y.N. Gumburg*; interior design — *I.G. Kuzmin*; structural engineers *S.V. Orlovsky* and *V.F. Michurin*. Block No. 3 — author *M.Y. Ginzburg*. Main staircase — author arch. *I.I. Leonidov*; structural engineer *N.D. Vishnevsky*. Administrative block — architect *V.V. Kalinin*; structural engineer *K.K. Antonov*. Boiler-house and laundry — architect *F.I. Yalovkin*; structural engineer *K.K. Antonov*. Preparation room / kitchen architects *Belyakov* and *V.V. Kalinin*. Site plan — *Y.M. Popov* and *V.V. Kalinin*. Layout of the park — *L.S. Zalesskaya*. Artists: *G.O. Rublev, N.P. Prussakov, V. Sokolov.* Sculptors: *A.E. Zelensky, A.G. Sotnikov.* Furniture engineer — *G. Belitsky.* Sanitary-technical works: head eng. *A.I. Shneyerov*, eng. *I.I. Volfovich* and *N.V. Bukharina.* Treatment block and interior equipment for the sanatorium: sanatorium director — *Dr. M.M. Bolotner* and *F.L. Konstantinovskaya.* Head of construction and principal engineer — *A.P. Nekrasov.* Deputy principal engineer, head of works section — *N.D. Vishnevsky.* Head of 2nd site — *G.B. Tarsis.* Head of Santekhstroy office — *A.M. Nayda.* Head of Stroyelektro office — *Gordon.* Head of marble and cladding works — *P.V. Strakhov.* Treatment block — author architect *I.I. Shpalek*, structural engineers — *S.V. Orlovsky* and *A.A. Alendorf*, consultant — *Dr. I.D. Yakhnin.* Deputy head of construction — *V.F. Litvinov.* Photographs — *G.E. Sanko.*

INTRODUCTION

Enshrined in the greatest historic document of mankind, the Stalinist Constitution, are the remarkable victories of the socialist revolution, as well as victories and successes in building socialism in our country.

In the country of socialism, exploitation of man by man has been destroyed forever, labour has become a matter of glory, honour, valour and heroism, and every possible condition has been created for the wonderful growth and development in culture, science and art.

In the great country of socialism, every worker is guaranteed the right to education, labour, a comfortable old age and recreation.

The socialist revolution has created a new, socialist, man — the man of the great Stalinist epoch who requires of science, technology and art the satisfaction of his new needs, needs which are growing with every day.

From the very first years of the socialist revolution Soviet architecture, one of the most important and complex fields of human activity, has faced tasks which are extraordinary in their scope and importance.

How to create and design in detail new types and forms of public buildings and structures as well as new types of industrial buildings for socialist labour, how to lay out socialist cities, how to create the new style, that of the architecture of socialism — these are some of the universal creative tasks confronting Soviet architecture.

One of the most important of these numerous creative tasks is the question of the architecture of socialist-type sanatoria and houses of recreation, buildings which are a striking embodiment of the great care Stalin shows towards the people.

A distinctive characteristic of the socialist type of sanatorium is that it should embody Stalin's care for people in a profound synthetic unity of elements with diverse functions. Such elements are, for instance, residential rooms and groups of communal, treatment and service rooms. The organic link between these groups, and how they combine and interact with their different functions, should be expressed and embodied in the unity of the architectural organism.

To realize this large and complex creative challenge in its entirety was the task set by the creative team, led by architecture professor M.Y. Ginzburg, in designing the NKTP [People's Commissariat for Heavy Industry] sanatorium in Kislovodsk.

The team's creative efforts and quests went beyond merely architectural and spatial objectives, or narrowly utilitarian and practical issues; they were directed at tackling the entire aggregate of issues, from the careful choice of the sanatorium's location and planning of the site layout to the design of individual parts of the fittings and decoration; moreover, the desire to achieve the style of socialist realism as far as possible was a fundamental principle in the team's creative work.

The architectural embodiment of Stalin's care for people; a sincerity and truthfulness of expression, involving an organic connection and congruence between form and content that stems from an in-depth elaboration of form; a simplicity and laconicism of expression (qualities that have little in common with the meagreness of asceticism); the quest for a distinctive language unique to this style — these are the main principles in the understanding of the style of socialist realism which guided the creative team led by professor M.Y. Ginzburg in their work.

A clear appreciation of these aspirations, this creative credo, was undoubtedly instrumental in the design of the NKTP sanatorium, helping to impart a fundamental coherence to the creative concept as a whole as well as to individual details and elements.

While I do not set myself the goal in this short introduction of giving an analysis or critique of the architectural design of the NKTP sanatorium in Kislovodsk in general, it nevertheless seems necessary to note as a positive phenomenon the profound and extraordinary attention paid by the authors of this project to tying the ensemble of buildings to the site conditions and in particular to linking the building to the remarkable landscape and amazingly beautiful panorama of the Caucasian mountain range, which is crowned with the two snow-white peaks of Mount Elbrus. The fact that in both blocks all the residential rooms, without exception, are south-facing and protected from the winds, each having a window containing a perfectly composed landscape is, first, of great artistic significance in the composition of each room and, secondly, has important psychotherapeutic effects.

Noting the positive work done by the authors of the project in terms of the architectural conception of the Soviet sanatorium, I would nevertheless like to point out a residue of schematism in the structuring of the architectural volumes and forms, something most strongly manifested in the architecture of the special-regime blocks. In particular, in the design of the wall surfaces, the distribution of window apertures, loggias and so on we may trace echoes of the compositional techniques of the now defunct Constructivist style, with its tendency to simplify and its affectedness in demonstrating the 'functional' purpose of the building as a whole or of its constituent parts and elements.

In the whole complex of sanatorium buildings one of the most successful in terms of architectural design is the circular bath building. The special-regime blocks, which are highly important in terms of their significance for the life of the sanatorium, are more schematic in their forms and interpretation of details.

Very considerable importance in the architecture of the interiors — in particular, in the residential rooms — is given to particular items of equipment. Until recently, our construction industry supplied equipment conforming to old, obsolete and imperfect types and standards. Comrade S. Ordzhonikidze therefore decided to use the construction of the sanatorium to fight for the introduction of new and better manufacturing standards. To this end, almost all the items of equipment were specially designed by the team under professor M.Y. Ginzburg.

The result of this initiative by comrade Ordzhonikidze is that our construction industry has adopted many new types and standards; architects now have at their disposal numerous prototypes and items of equipment of the highest quality.

Just as important is the work done by professor M.Y. Ginzburg's creative team in designing types of furniture for the sanatorium. Studying and assimilating all the material on furniture which has accumulated over the last quarter of a century, both in the USSR and in other countries, has undoubtedly produced positive results. However, it must nevertheless be regretted that in designing certain parts of the wooden furniture, the architects have insufficiently — and insufficiently creatively — incorporated and assimilated the extremely rich material on furniture which has been left us by the 18th and 19th centuries.

As well as the architects, we should note the intrinsic role played by artists in the design of the sanatorium. The fact that artist-comrades Rublev, Prussakov and the team of V.A. Favorsky, and the sculptors Zelensky and Sotnikov were organically involved in the design work and in tackling a unitary spatial task has contributed greatly to the coherence of the designs for the interiors and to achieving a true synthesis of the arts.

The process of designing the sanatorium, which involved the full participation of the architect in elaborating all aspects of this multi-layered task through the architect's active, constant and daily participation on the building site and the realization of the slogan 'Architect, get up the scaffolding!', is one of the most positive examples in our extensive architectural and construction practice.

The authors of this book rightly and justifiably note in self-criticism a number of faults in their work, resulting mainly from the problem of architectural form and how to resolve and interpret this problem. The faults they have uncovered are to a certain extent common to all architectural practice today and mostly derive from the considerable delay in working through theoretical problems in Soviet architecture, in particular, and the issue of the style of socialist realism. The positive results which have been attained by the team of architects under the direction of M.Y. Ginzburg in designing and building the NKTP sanatorium in Kislovodsk are further evidence of the wonderful conditions which now exist for creative work in our great country; and of the successes which may be attained by a team of architects or an individual architect in those cases where they have proceeded along the path of true creative quest and have set themselves tasks which do not merely involve form, but are imbued throughout with ideological singleness of purpose.

This book is the best illustration of these attainments.

Architectural academician *N.Y. Kolli*

ARCHITECTURAL ISSUES

LANDSCAPE AND TERRAIN

Deep elongated ravines and valleys alternate with hills. The gullies are sheltered and are often covered in vegetation: spruce, pine and fruit trees. The green slopes of the hills either descend gently into a gully or break off abruptly in stony, yellow-red scarps, exposing Kislovodsk's geomorphological backbone.

Standing in a gully, you see only the hills in the foreground. As you climb, the horizon expands, revealing the region's natural structure in remarkable clarity. Behind the first chain of hills a second rises up, behind the second a third and then sometimes a fourth. The two snow-white peaks of Elbrus loom in the distance.

Man started settling these gullies and valleys long ago. Small houses, vegetable plots and gardens occupied secluded and well-protected spots.

With the October Revolution came a new developer, who erected grand and monumental edifices in Kislovodsk — palaces of health for workers: sanatoria and houses of recreation.

However, in most cases the new developer proceeded along a well-beaten path, filling the gullies and valleys with sanatorium buildings. If building up the gullies with small houses made sense, the construction of new sanatoria in the area below is less successful.

The gullies and valleys are becoming cluttered; the adjacent hills are losing their scale, their defined silhouette; the buildings themselves look inelegant; and with the rear facades of the buildings abutting so closely to the hills or cliffs, poorly ventilated, damp corridors are formed which are unfit for use (see the Gosbank and VTsSPS [All-Union Central Soviet of Trade Unions] sanatoria, and others).

For the construction of the NKTP sanatorium, comrade Sergo Ordzhonikidze personally chose a beautiful site in Rebrovaya Gully. Beyond this terrain are other areas of land, above the gully and opposite the Temple of Air. The upper plot of land was completely bare, while the lower part was covered in beautiful vegetation. It was for this reason, and likewise under the influence of local tradition, that we began designing the sanatorium on the lower plot of land.

However, the very first design we came up with convinced us that this was the wrong approach to take. A model was made of the buildings within the natural landscape, and all the negative aspects of this option were immediately clear. The several versions that followed, with mixed development on the top and at the bottom, also proved unsatisfactory since they failed to eliminate entirely the drawbacks of having buildings on the lower plot.

Finally, we switched to developing purely the top area. This approach initially seemed highly risky, since we were worried by the lack of vegetation on the site and by the amount of wind. However, this course of action turned out to be more correct. It was possible to take the edge off the winds, and even, in several south-facing locations, create areas completely protected from the wind. The planting of vegetation on the upper plateau in coming years will further change its climate.

In the final analysis it was this version that best provided the sanatorium with landscape, sun, air and extensive open spaces.

[3]

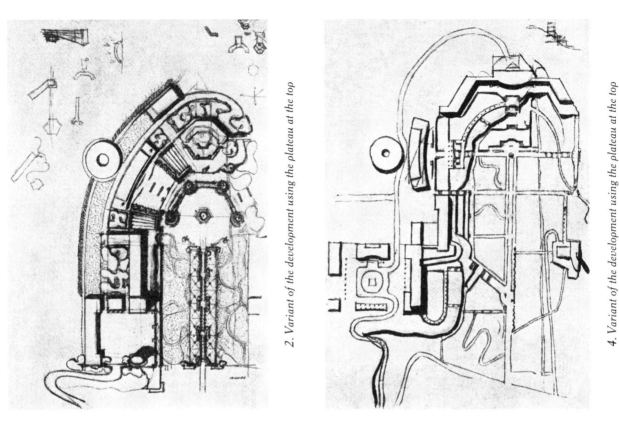

2. *Variant of the development using the plateau at the top*

4. *Variant of the development using the plateau at the top*

1. *Variant of the development using some of the plateau at the top and some of the lower part of the site*

3. *Variant of the development using the plateau at the top*

[4]

5. *General view of the Georgievskoe Plateau and Kislovodsk following construction of the sanatorium*

ISSUES RELATING TO SPATIAL COMPOSITION

The main elements in the sanatorium's spatial composition are three blocks: the two special-regime blocks (nos. 1 and 2) and the treatment block. The entire composition should come across, on first sight, as an easily legible pattern, its complexity gradually revealing itself on closer examination. Due to its functional structure as a sanatorium, the emphasis was on a compositional pattern and optical symmetry that achieves equilibrium through the main dimensions of the elevation and governing principles, but is entirely distinct in the articulations and elements of the buildings themselves.

The main axis of the composition clearly had to be the treatment block. With such an important function, the block's architectural structure was also predetermined.

While in general a sanatorium's treatment block occupies a less prominent position, in our project it plays a special role because it combines every type of modern treatment available, making this one of the most advanced treatment institutions in the USSR and Europe.

The two elevations which balance this axis are the two special-regime blocks, nos 1 and 2. Block no. 1 consists of single and double rooms, while block no. 2 comprises two-room apartments. In order to balance block no. 2 with an elevation of the same dimensions, the double rooms in block no. 1 jut out from the line of the facade. Thus the core of the composition comprises the following: the treatment block in the centre; the double rooms of special-regime block no. 1 to the west; and special-regime block no. 2 to the east.

The full extent of the composition is oriented towards the southern horizon and that part of Kislovodsk which is most interesting in terms of its landscape.

The two special-regime blocks form the equivalent of two wings extending towards the southern horizon and embracing the entire panorama of the mountains, with Elbrus in the centre. This means that all the residential rooms in these two wings are south-facing and have a window framing a perfect landscape composition. It is this window framing the landscape that is undoubtedly the most important factor in the artistic resolution of each room's composition.

The decoration and furnishing of the rooms are entirely subordinated to this main device of framing the landscape; they should be seen as elements that supplement this idea.

Finally, an important role in the overall spatial composition is played by the consideration given to the terrain of the Georgievskoe Plateau, on which the sanatorium has been built.

[5]

Due to its structure, the plateau forms a gentler fold between two precipitous cliffs that descends to the lower park area of the site. It seemed only natural to make this fold the axis of the entire composition: the treatment block was placed here, and the main staircase linking the top part of the site with the bottom starts from here. The staircase is built in the form of an amphitheatre on top of the terrain of the fold. It links the two sides of the sheer cliffs with the top and bottom parts of the plateau. However, an entirely consistent approach was not possible because the axis of this naturally formed composition does not continue into the lower park; indeed, it is set at a different angle to the axis formed by the magnificent alley of ancient shade-giving spruce trees.

We were unable completely to overcome the contradiction that exists between these compositional axes in the two natural landscapes of the top and bottom terrains. The continuation of the main staircase in the lower part of the park develops not along the amphitheatre's principal axis, but along one of the subsidiary sub-axes of the semicircular niche. While this creates the impression of an entirely consistent and compositionally logical development of the entire motif at the top and on the staircase itself, at the bottom, however, and on the alley in the lower park, the task remains not quite finished. Several additional measures are needed to smooth over the sharpest corners of this most difficult compositional challenge.

Another extremely difficult task was to determine where the buildings should end in relation to the line where the cliff breaks off. Should we move them right up to the cliff edge or push them back away from the edge? And if we were to push them back, how far? Only after a number of demarcation tests in the field was it possible to find an answer. To move the buildings right up to the cliff edge would have been impermissible. If the height of the adjacent cliffs had

6. Site layout for the sanatorium

[6]

7. Panoramic view of the sanatorium from the Temple of the Air

been notably greater than the height of the buildings, this would have been the most effective and mutually successful way to reveal the scales of both the cliff and the buildings in relation to one another. As it is, the cliffs are of no great height and their impressive scale results from the various fissure lines and the texture of the rocks.

All it would take is to move the facades of the five-storey structures right up to the edge of these cliffs for their scale to be destroyed in an instant — and without any benefit in terms of the grandness of scale of the buildings. But by moving the buildings some distance back from the cliff edge, to the point where the base of the buildings are not immediately visible from below — in other words back into the middle ground — and at the same time revealing this base to a sufficient extent, we arrive at the most correct solution. The cliffs do not merely retain their scale and picturesque qualities to the full, they also seem larger and more picturesque than the architecture, which is visible only in the middle ground.

This approach has the effect of making the buildings appear larger in scale.

Furthermore, the sanatorium is enriched by the new areas of open space that are thus created between the building facades and the cliff edge. These areas are protected from the winds and lit by the southern sun.

They are enclosed between the austere lines of the buildings and the soft folds of the Caucasian range, where the contrast between the geometrical shapes of the architecture and nature's fluid forms fully reveals and emphasises their divergent qualities.

Together with the amphitheatre of the staircase, which is their continuation, these south-facing areas in front of the sanatorium's main blocks become the most attractive place for patients to relax in.

By contrast, the natural conditions in the northern part of the Georgievskoe Plateau are entirely different. The slope itself, unlike the south-facing slope, is not particularly steep, descending to Budennovskaya

Gully in considerably more gentle fashion. This north side reveals a different type of landscape. Instead of the many various depths of view which unfold on the south side, here the mountains fill the horizon with their laconic and austere silhouette.

This explains why different principles of development have been adopted here, principles that correlate to the character of the small two-storey ancillary structures on this side.

The entire composition of the north side is based on the principle of free equilibrium, organized on a single axis of symmetry between the two identical blocks of the administrative building. The gap between these blocks reveals the outline of the mountains to the north and, to the south, the axis of the entrance to the main block and the parterre with a pool and a fountain. The other service structures take the form of a terrace (the roof of the garage, for instance, serves as a courtyard space for the food-preparation room and laundry). The ensemble of buildings ends in a retaining wall which runs along the entire north slope.

Visitors, as they drive up to Budennovka and arrive at the foot of the north slope, perceive the gently sloping face of the mountain and the terrace-like composition of the buildings as a coherent whole. The buildings finish and crown the slope, becoming part of its silhouette. At various turns in the road and at different angles this composition becomes more distinct, dominating the mountain slope. The driveway leading into the open area between the blocks of the administrative building, the landscape of the mountains, and the fountains should reinforce the impression of a coherent composition.

But the strongest visual impressions are yet to come. After visitors complete the usual registration procedures and finally arrive at their rooms, they are met with a wonderful surprise: the landscape to the south and the sun-flooded panorama of the Caucasian mountains. Only then do they appreciate the setting in which their recreation is to be spent.

RESIDENTIAL ROOMS

The brief given to us by comrade Sergo Ordzhonikidze, the initiator and inspirer of the sanatorium's construction, required us not so much to create a typical sanatorium establishment as to work on the image of a new socialist sanatorium that would enshrine the material and cultural attainments of the Soviet regime over the 20 years of its existence and determine the directions in which our construction practices should develop for at least several years to come.

In a building such as a sanatorium these aspirations needed, above all, to be realized as fully as

possible in the broadest sense of health, in a review of all existing standards, and in adjusting these standards to take account of guests' true needs. Above all, they needed to be reflected in the type of room available as accommodation.

The sanatorium's location at the top of the Georgievskoe Plateau, outside the city and higher than all the city's buildings, made it possible to fulfil this objective as fully as possible. Those who come for recreation are, above all, provided with an abundance of air which is rarefied, ozone-rich and clean.

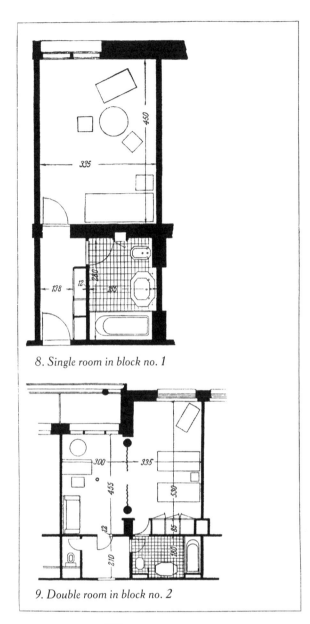

8. Single room in block no. 1

9. Double room in block no. 2

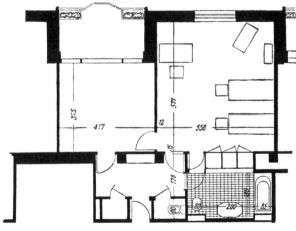

10. Space for a single family in block no. 2

Professor Kalitin recently conducted research into the cleanliness of the air at the Semashko sanatorium, which is much lower than the NKTP sanatorium and closer to the city centre. The air there turned out to be significantly purer than at the bottom, in the Narzan Gallery.

Applying these findings to our sanatorium, located at a greater height above sea level, we may confidently say that patients are surrounded here by a bottomless reservoir of pure, ozonized air containing almost no microbes or dust. Similarly, there are more hours of sunshine here, less humidity, and an almost complete absence of mist. We have often had occasion to observe an extremely interesting scene: the entire city and Budennovskaya and Rebrovaya gullies lying enveloped in a seamless veil of white mist, while the Georgievskoe Plateau and sanatorium buildings above are lit up by the sun.

I should add that each room has a view of the southern horizon. The beautiful landscape creates important psychotherapeutic effects.

Comrade Ordzhonikidze took a great deal of interest in the dimensions of the residential rooms.

The floor area adopted as minimal for a room in the residential blocks is 15 m². This comfortably accommodates a bed, table, chairs and an armchair in which to relax, and there is space left over. Apart from the bed, there may also be a sofa. The room's height is 3.5 m. The room is very spacious, having a cubic volume of 52.5 m³. Occupying such a room has a positive effect on the patient's psyche.

Each residential room in the sanatorium has its own sanitary-technical unit.

Some rooms in this same block are intended for two patients. These consist of two residential spaces separated from one another by columns and a curtain. One of the spaces has two beds, a night table, a washstand with a console mirror, an armchair, upholstered stools for changing clothes, and built-in cupboards for clothes and linen. The other space contains armchairs, a desk and a sofa and may be used as a living room or study. Here there are three ancillary spaces: an entrance area, a bathroom and a toilet.

In his desire to provide the best conditions for the recreation and treatment of workers of the People's Commissariat for Heavy Industry, who are overburdened with important work, comrade Sergo Ordzhonikidze proposed designing a further type of residential space intended for families with children. Rooms of this type are to be found in block no. 2. These consist of a bedroom, a living room, a storage cupboard, an entrance area and a corridor.

An important issue in residential spaces is the light aperture as a source of sunlight and air.

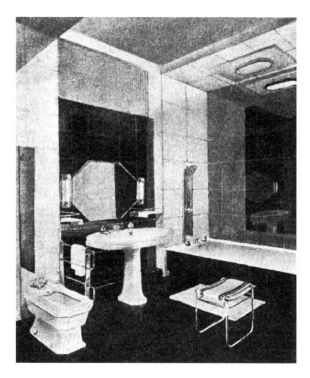

11. Bathroom attached to residential rooms in blocks 1 and 2

For this reason, we strove to make the windows as large as possible.

At the same time, given the southern orientation of the residential spaces, it was necessary to avoid the rooms becoming badly overheated. Thus the character and size of the window aperture were determined by the individual conditions governing the location of the particular room. In those cases where a room's window had the floor of a terrace above, with the terrace blocking some of the rays of the sun, the window aperture was made as large as possible. Where there was no terrace of this kind, the window aperture was made smaller.

12. Fittings in a bathroom in blocks 1 and 2

The terraces for all the residential rooms are between 3 and 5 m² in dimension. This makes it possible to put a bed on the terrace.

To begin with, it was intended that the terraces should be shared by several rooms. Comrade Ordzhonikidze condemned this 'un-socialist' approach, as he called it, and demanded that each room without exception should have a completely separate terrace protected from the gaze of others.

This means that the terraces are now a constituent part of the rooms.

All the above are essential hygienic and sanitary-technical preconditions which have to be met by residential units in a socialist sanatorium.

We have tried to give patients the greatest degree of c o m f o r t in the residential spaces and to satisfy all their needs as fully as possible, and in the broadest possible sense.

Everything that might be found in the residential spaces of a sanatorium over and above this, in other words elements of superfluous luxury, we rejected.

For this reason the internal decoration of the residential spaces is characterized by great simplicity and is primarily based on quality materials and on careful execution of work. There are almost no moulded decorations. The ceiling mouldings are simple and understated, and merely set out to organically articulate the walls and ceiling.

The colours used for the walls are everywhere exceedingly restrained, in various shades of yellow, pink, light blue and green. The use of distemper on an oil undercoat gives an even and velvety colour.

The walls of the bedrooms in the double rooms and in the apartments in block no. 2 have fitted cupboards for clothes and linen; these are concealed behind wooden panels. They are extremely simple in their detailing and patterns, but their natural texture gives them a sense of refinement, and a considerable element of softness and intimacy is thus introduced.

We paid a great deal of attention to the interior design of the bathrooms. Our aim was not just to equip them with maximum comfort, but also to create a setting that would make washing and taking care of their bodies particularly enjoyable for patients.

The walls of the single room's bathroom are painted with oil paint. The floors are laid with Mettlach tiles. The bath, washbasin, mirror and toilet are conveniently placed.

The bathrooms in the other residential rooms are more spacious. Their walls are faced in black and white marblite, with the baths likewise clad in marblite.

The mirror-like surface of the black marblite, the mirror, the white marblite, and the nickel fittings, which enliven the colour scheme of the room, give the interiors of the bathrooms a very

13. Room furnishings

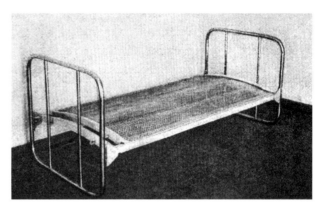

16. Bed

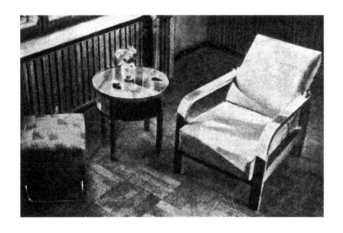

14. Room furnishings

17. Sofa-bed

15. Room furnishings

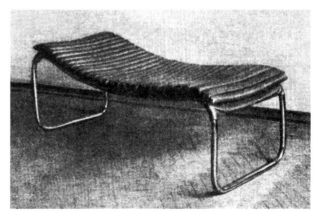

18. Chaise-longue for terraces

[11]

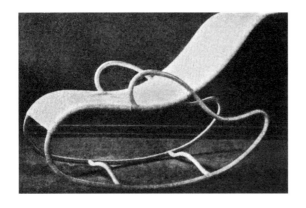

19. Chaise-longue for terraces

22. Table

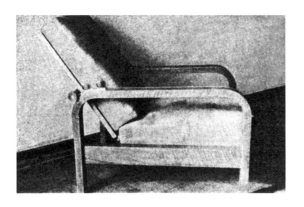

20. Armchair

23. Desk

21. A quiet spot in one of the rooms

24. Small table

25. Night-table with drawers

[12]

smart appearance. The human body is reflected repeatedly in the mirror surfaces of the walls. The setting itself compels patients to take care of their hygiene.

In designing the interiors of the residential rooms particular care has been given to ensuring the highest level of standards for the equipment. We paid a great deal of attention to this issue, and comrade Sergo Ordzhonikidze and S.E. Ginzburg, head of Glavstroyprom, decided to use the construction of the sanatorium as an opportunity to have obsolete standards dropped from production. For this reason we specially designed and commissioned almost all elements of the equipment. This included: standards for the faience in the bathrooms and toilets, taps and mixer taps for baths and washbasins, handles for doors and cupboards, hinges for windows and doors, window fastenings, fuses, switches, sockets, electric-light fixtures, and so on.

When compared to ordinary factory production, all these objects stand out in a fairly favourable light; they introduce certain new characteristics into the interiors of the residential accommodation.

The character of a residential room largely depends on the type of furniture. The invention of new types of furniture, however, would entail an enormous amount of labour.

Following a prolonged period of planning, we concluded that it was necessary to confine our work to studying and assimilating all the material on furniture that had accumulated over the last quarter of a century, both in the USSR and in other countries.

In the final analysis, the style of the furniture was encapsulated in objects which are simple and pure in shape and proportions and which optimally fulfil their various functions, satisfying the aesthetic needs of the patient both in terms of materials and execution.

We became convinced that even with such a brief there was broad scope for architects to exercise their creativity and the work required was likely to be very labour-intensive.

In terms of choice of material and basic structure, it was decided to design furniture of three types — from wood, metal and wicker.

For the single rooms the furniture is entirely made from wood.

In order to avoid cluttering the room with a large amount of furniture, and to afford patients the opportunity to lie down during the day, we concluded that it was necessary to design a transformable sofa-bed. American and Western-European practice provides numerous examples of designs for fold-away beds which can be raised during the day and which are installed in a corresponding niche

in the wall or cupboard. An example of this is the accommodation in the international sleeping coach, where the bed turns on its axis. However, in all these cases the transformation is extremely complex and requires a fairly significant expenditure of physical effort. Furthermore, these beds are not always entirely hygienic.

The sofa-bed in the single room in our sanatorium consists of a sofa whose back is a mattress. At the head of the bed is a ventilated drawer for storing bed belongings; this drawer takes the form of a night table. At night the mattress is spread out on the sofa and the bed belongings, which are kept in a special bag, are taken out of the drawer. Making the bed takes 2—3 minutes.

Another serious task was the choice of type of table. In discussing this issue, comrade Sergo Ordzhonikidze strongly objected to the use of a stereotypical desk that would give the residential room too much of an official character. So we used a circular table with just a single drawer for writing materials.

We opted for a type of chair with a back which can be tilted at any angle, allowing patients to sit, recline or semi-recline. A small round table beside the sofa and two chairs complete the furnishing of the single room.

A great deal of care went into selecting the texture of the wood, and the relation between the colour of the upholstery and curtains and the colour of the rooms in general. All the wooden furniture is covered with nitro varnish; this is extremely convenient since nitro varnish is relatively strong, making it possible to wash and clean the furniture with ease.

For the bedroom in the double rooms and the apartments in block no. 2 we chose a metal bed with an elastic mesh and a revertex mattress.

This also determined the style of the furniture in the bedroom, all of which has a metal frame — a practice which is fairly common in America and in the West (there are also instances where it has been used in the USSR).

We studied the experience of the best-known furniture firms and used this research to develop our own types of metal furniture. The key decision was to use steel tubes, which are particularly light and flexible. In our country metal gas pipes are generally used to make metal furniture; the result is both heavy and clumsy. The problem with chairs and armchairs of this type is that they are rigid and inconvenient because they have no flexibility.

Instead, it proved possible to make the metal furniture from steel pipes discarded by the aviation industry. The seat and armrests of the armchair are covered in dense fabric or leather in various bright colours.

The bedrooms of the double rooms and apartments in block no. 2 are furnished exclusively with metal furniture (beds, night tables, console mirrors with toilettes, upholstered chairs). The living room has wooden furniture upholstered in coloured fabrics. The fact that a single space in the apartment has two types of furniture made of contrasting materials does not violate the overall impression, since the same general approach has been taken to issues relating to the furniture's style.

Pliable wicker has been used to make the tables, chaise-longues, armchairs and chairs. The same material decorates the terraces and loggias.

It proved possible to make some of the fabrics for the curtains and upholstering materials at factories to specially commissioned designs, but most of the fabrics had to be selected from the range of materials that was already in production, changing only the colours.

These, therefore, are the key aspects behind the design of the residential rooms in the sanatorium: a totality of means determining their character and style. We are convinced that there is no need for other means by which to tackle this task. A passion for rich mouldings, a revival of historical styles, and the inclination for magnificence and superfluous luxury can only turn architects away from the path of socialist realism.

FACTORS RELATING TO TREATMENT

A systematic examination of patients is the key principle that underlies treatment at the sanatorium. To this end use is made of the most modern equipment.

The sanatorium has a biochemical laboratory. The most notable pieces of equipment in this laboratory are the Pulfrich photometer, the latest model of the Zeiss-Icon hemometer, magnificent Miflex microscopes with universal photographic cameras and drawing devices, a very interesting and clever capillaroscope with a small photo-camera, a device for determining gas exchange with a kymograph, and an electrocardiograph.

An especially important instrument among the scientific-research equipment is the Tuto-Helio-phos X-ray machine. This is fitted with an X-ray kymograph, making it possible to photograph organs while they are moving, and with a kymoscope into which the X-ray kymogram may be inserted. With the help of a complex system of mirrors and a moving prism the observer sees the organ being studied, in movement. A universal tripod — a tele-nantoscope — makes it possible to conduct transillumination and to take photographs regardless of the patient's position. The Albrecht explurator can be used to carry out all kinds of investigations of internal organs. It is possible to switch instantly from simple transillumination to taking serial photographs.

In addition, investigations of patients make use of a number of interesting devices needed by otorhinolaryngologists, ophthalmologists, hygienologists and urologists.

Baths with Narzan mineral water are available in a special block which is part of the sanatorium's treatment building. Extensive use is made of hydrotherapy (the sanatorium has a swimming pool) and electrotherapy involving all kinds of treatment, including ultrashort waves — the latest scientific development in this field.

Next, mention should be made of recuperative PE and mechanotherapy. The sanatorium has acquired a large number of devices providing the most diverse types of treatment (a double bicycle; a double rowing machine with a counter; vibrators for massaging the stomach, the entire body and all parts of a limb; apparatuses for exercising the muscles of the arms and spine; a gymnastic apparatus for correcting stoops, etc.).

The sanatorium makes use of all types of inhalation, including inhalation of rarefied air. There is a superbly equipped dental treatment room. A number of the latest devices have been acquired for hydrotherapy. The sanatorium also has equipment for treating patients who work in mines, at open-hearth furnaces, and at chemical factories, as well as patients suffering from professional diseases.

The sanatorium thus provides not just scientific investigation and treatment of patients, but also opportunities for scientific medical research.

This multiplicity of treatment methods adopted in the sanatorium thus required the creation of a special treatment block and also influenced how the block was fitted out.

Our aim was to make the treatment block — the sanatorium's central building — as little like a hospital as possible in terms of its external appearance. We strove to make it so clean, smart, welcoming and even homely that the treatment procedures would not vex the patient, and patients would come to experience conditioned reflexes that would facilitate treatment and rest.

For this reason all the rooms in the treatment block are full of air, sun and light, and the colours of the finishings are bright and uplifting.

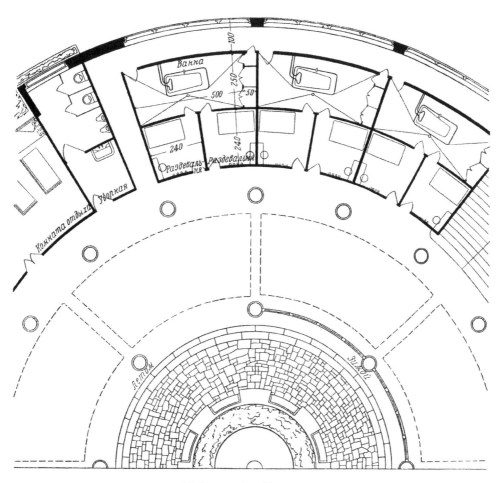

26. Section of the Narzan baths

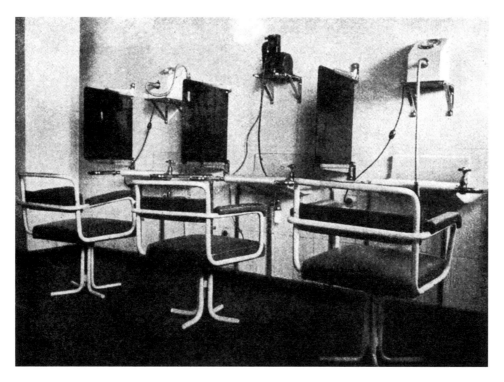

27. The inhalation room

[15]

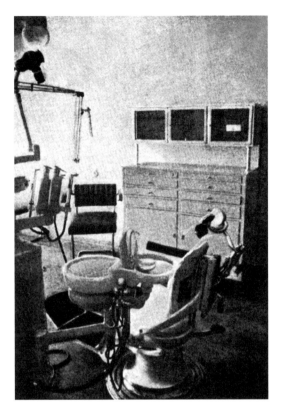

28. Equipment in a dental treatment room

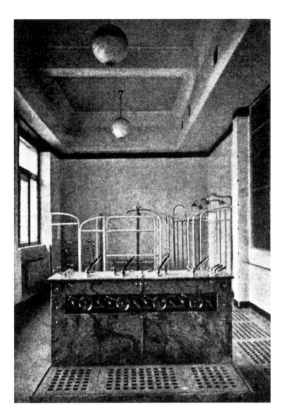

29. Podium in a hydrotherapy room

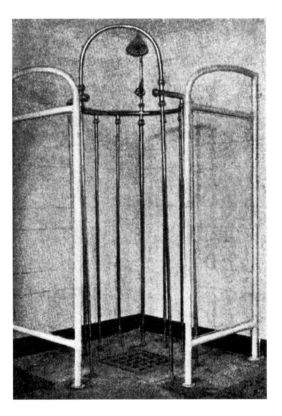

30. Mantel shower in a hydrotherapy room

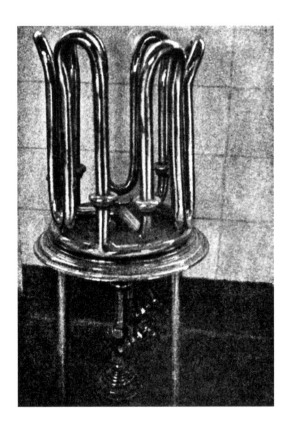

31. Radiator for drying sheets in a hydrotherapy room

32. Armchair for the vestibule in the treatment block

33. Armchair for the vestibule in the treatment block

34. Sofa for the vestibule in the treatment block

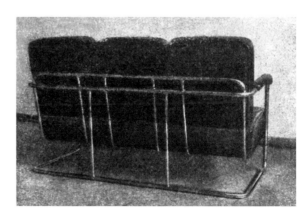

35. Sofa for the vestibule in the treatment block

Enormous importance has been given to the treatment block's entrance hall, which is the first impression visitors receive when they enter the building. The walls, floor and main staircase of the hall are faced in very light, almost white, Koelga marble. Opposite the staircase a decorative panel by the artists Rublev and Prusakov is likewise in very light colours. The overall colour scheme of the hall's finishings is subtly warmed by the cinnabar in some of the squares of the flat ceiling caissons.

Enormous windows on the south side reveal a fine view of the Temple of Air and the Caucasian Ridge.

The treatment rooms, which are decorated in a much simpler fashion, are full of light and not unattractive.

A beautiful feature of the rooms is the metal furniture upholstered with brightly coloured leather.

The central part of the treatment block is circular. Inside is an open courtyard with a fountain and baths of Narzan water placed around the outer ring. Narzan baths provide the main treatment procedure at Kislovodsk. We have done everything possible to create an interior which facilitates the

37. Refrigeration cabinets

38. Fittings in the kitchen pantry

healing effects of the Narzan baths. Above all, the building's enlarged dimensions create a great sense of space. The blue sky of Kislovodsk fits perfectly into the circle of the inner courtyard, making it seem as if the dividing line between inner space and nature has been erased. All this helps to make the interior very light and spatially vibrant. The mosaic floor contains rhythmically designed inserts of separate medallions made from marble mosaic, with images of fish, seahorses, starfish and snails. The circular crowning frieze above the glass of the inner courtyard is to be faced with a coloured composition made from faience (by the artist Rublev and the sculptor Sotnikov), depicting doves against a background of sky and greenery.

The sanatorium's flat roofs provide a vast supplementary area where patients can walk and undergo aerotherapy and heliotherapy. When creeping plants (ivy, vines, wisteria) are added and canvas tents are installed here, it will be possible to use the roofs during winter and summer at any time of day.

36. The kitchen in block no. 2

An extremely important part of the service provided at the sanatorium is f o o d.

Both residential blocks have separate dining rooms. All the household processes which can be moved out of the main residential blocks without too much difficulty are concentrated in a special food-preparation/canteen block. Here there is a central refrigeration complex, a series of rooms for preparing and storing food, a canteen and kitchen for service staff, a bakery and a confectionery section. The residential blocks contain cooking rooms, preparation rooms, sinks, buffets, refrigeration cabinets and rooms for service staff

All the rooms are very light and well ventilated. Rooms intended for wet processes have floors made from metal tiles and walls faced with glazed tiles. The food-preparation processes are electrified.

The dining rooms in the residential blocks are smart, but at the same time simple. The landscape plays an important role in the location of the dining rooms and in their architectural character. The dining room in block no. 2 has two large glass windows with metal transoms on its east and west sides. On the east side the entire window is filled with the silhouette of the mountains and the open area with flowerbeds and a fountain; the window on the west side reveals a complex combination formed by the architectural volumes of the treatment and main blocks. The contrast between these two landscapes gives the dining room its special charm.

The dining room in the main block stretches out along the south facade and is much larger. It is likewise illuminated from two sides, but here it is the south side with its varied landscape that is the more important. Alongside the dining room is a closed terrace, which serves as its extension. Slightly lower down is a second, open, terrace.

ROOMS FOR PATIENTS' RECREATION

A number of rooms at the sanatorium are intended for patients to relax in. This is the purpose not just of special rooms such as the living rooms and billiard rooms, but of all the ancillary spaces (entrance halls, corridors, terraces, flat roofs, and so on). Given that patients are constantly passing through and along the entrance halls and corridors, we tried to make sure that the decoration of these spaces should feel as spacious as possible while also maximising their use, and making them feel cozy.

The entrance hall of the main block consists of an enfilade of rooms which runs, mirroring a terrace, from north to south. This hall is structured as a strictly axial composition.

The entrance hall of block no. 2 is much more intimate and comprises an unusual kind of winter garden. The two large glazed surfaces frame a beautiful landscape. Its remaining surfaces have a deliberately coarse garden type of texture. The plinths and columns are faced in dolomite; the floor is covered in gravel and merely edged in marble; in the centre of the room is a flowerbed; along the walls are special boxes with flowers planted in them; one wall has a niche containing a fountain and a pool.

In our opinion, the interior of this space is extremely successful.

Looking from the large corridor windows, wonderful landscapes extend towards the north. Widenings and niches in the corridors eliminate any monotony and serve as small living rooms. All the corridors are lined with wooden panels made from nut, oak, sycamore, elm and other woods.

While the living rooms, billiard rooms and other public spaces are inextricably linked in character and style with the entrance halls and corridors, the cinema and concert hall are in a different style altogether. In dimensions alone, this hall stands out from the other rooms. Its walls are faced in marble, some of which is white (Koelga), some Tagil and in certain parts red (Shrosha). Two rows of fluted white columns divide the room into three parts — a middle part which is wider, and side parts which are narrower. The level of the floor in the middle part is two steps lower than the floor level in the side parts. During concerts or film showings upholstered chairs are placed in the middle part and small tables and armchairs in the side parts.

PRINCIPAL TECHNICAL SOLUTIONS. DECORATION AND CLADDING WORK

The main technical specifications adopted for different parts of the sanatorium at Kislovodsk derived from the desire to ensure that the load-bearing structures should be perfect and long-lasting, and that the decorative and facing materials used should be of high quality.

All the main load-bearing structures and floor/ceiling structures are of reinforced concrete. The caisson or small-rib floor/ceiling structures used for the sanatorium are often employed as elements in the architectural structure of the ceiling.

The sanatorium's flat woodchip-and-cement roofs are covered on the outside with sand and terrazzo slabs. The system of drainpipes will be discussed below.

The window transoms are of oak, while the doors are of different types of hardwood. Rooms used for treatments involving water have floors made of metal tiles and walls faced in glazed tiles. Bathrooms, rooms intended for hydrotherapy, and the swimming pool have walls lined with black and white marblite. Metal parts are chrome-plated.

For the facing of the internal walls in some rooms use has been made of hardwood or marble (Koelga, Byuk-Yankoy, Ufaley, Shrosha, Tagil). With limited previous experience in using these precious materials, we embarked on the cladding work with caution. For this reason I would like to share our experience in this field.

After carrying out a number of tasks, we came to the conclusion that these precious materials are very impressive when used in small quantities, but not when they are used throughout. An especially impressive effect may be obtained when surfaces highlight the contrast between more expensive and simpler materials — matt and shiny, rough and polished, cold and warm.

In the main block the corridors of the double rooms are lined entirely in hardwood. The walls seem monotonous, and the wood comes across as an ordinary material. In the same block, in the corridors of the single rooms, hardwoods are used only for the lower parts and the profiled frames of the double doorways, which are situated rhythmically along the corridor. This is much more impressive. The rhythmical elements emphasised by the wood look much more architectural. Used in small quantities, wood can be a precious and attractive material, while the contrast between polished wood and the matt coloured surface of the wall paint brings out the specific qualities of both textures.

In this way the correct use of wood in an interior, and its effect, does not depend on its abundance.

39. Sandstone stonework
with strips of dolomite

40. Dolomite which has been rough-dressed
and worked using a tooth axe

41. Cyclopean stonework using dolomite

42. Sandstone stonework in the restraining wall

[21]

Often a positive result may be attained by using the material in small quantities. A slender string course of wood and several small panels made of a hardwood create an impression of extreme smartness and richness in those cases where they are used correctly and incisively from the point of view of the overall architectonic structure of the room — when the texture of the wood has been selected with an understanding of its nature and the wood has been given a profile which suits it perfectly. The treatment of the surface of the wood is also highly important. The use of a shiny polished surface is by no means always apt. In many cases a matt surface which has been treated with wax looks much more inviting and modest. Admittedly, wood coated with a nitro varnish is economically sensible as it remains in good condition for longer, but in large quantities this coating creates an unartistic impression since great expanses of glossy surface have an extraordinarily crude sheen to them. For this reason, in the sanatorium we used nitro varnish only for the furniture, where the wooden surfaces are of no great size and where the issue of length of service life is especially important.

The same issues arise likewise with regard to the marble cladding. Large surfaces of marble very often look worse than small ones. Marble of a red colour (Shrosha), which is not very attractive in large quantities, looks very beautiful when used as individual string courses or profiles in combination with other materials. For instance, in the concert hall in the main block this type of marble, used in combination with large surfaces of white marble (Koelga), makes a good impression.

Grey Ufaley marble is not attractive in large expanses. Yet, in the circular room with the Narzan baths, where it is used against a background of the uniformily coloured surface of the profiled architraves, it makes a favourable impression. Sometimes the marble edging of a surface or the covering of a part of a surface with marble fragments looks more effective than a large area of wall or floor lined entirely with marble. An especially good impression is made by harmoniously combining different types of marble, where one marble serves as the background and another as the frame, edging or profiling. In general, in facing works (using coloured wood and

43. The architectural appearance of the treatment block

44. *The winter garden in block no. 2*

marble) especial importance attaches to the careful selection of materials and the right relation between the materials and the quality of their installation. Of crucial importance is the join between pieces of the material; this should be as even and minimal as possible. If these requirements cannot be met, it may be better not to use these materials in case their positive qualities become transformed into their opposite.

In just the same way, the external cladding turned out to be an extremely serious problem for us. It is very important to use local cladding materials. These materials, apart from being cheap, impart to a building an organic unity with the surrounding landscape, due to their geological origin.

Indeed, yellow dolomite, the stone which is quarried in the vicinity of Kislovodsk, will always, under any circumstances, fit into the landscape

46. Part of the south facade of block no. 2

45. View of block no. 1

[24]

47. Pergola on the roof of block no. 2

48. Part of the interior view of the courtyard in the baths building

49. Faience frieze, details; artist: Rublev; sculptor: Sotnikov

of the surrounding mountains, as something that is an integral part of the latter. Choosing dolomite for the external cladding of the main blocks, we used yellow plaster of the same shade as the natural dolomite.

After carefully studying the ways in which dolomite has been used in the best old buildings, we came to the conclusion that the main condition for the correct application of cladding is a dry and slender, smooth, thread-like join between individual quadrels and slabs of dolomite. Slabs of dolomite of identical size were used, while the quadrels were of several different sizes, and use was also made of polygonal stonework, i.e. a mosaic of slabs of various irregular shapes, and then of so-called 'Armenian' stonework. The dolomite was worked using a bush hammer, bouchard and toothed chisel, and was employed rough-faced in a variety of reliefs. Each of these methods has its own architectural character.

However, at the same time we should not forget that sometimes a surface area of no great size faced in natural stone, in combination with plaster of a well selected texture, has given a better result than continuous cladding in dolomite.

Cladding with a natural material performs well in terms of service life. Although dolomite darkens with age and becomes covered in various stain marks, it does not lose any of its artistic expressiveness.

The walls of the garage and storage spaces, like some of the retaining walls, are clad with irregularly shaped pieces of local sandstone. Where the stonework has open joins, this cladding too stands out for its numerous artistic merits.

Combining different methods of cladding using local natural materials with coloured plaster opens up enormous artistic opportunities for architects.

ISSUES RELATING TO SOCIALIST REALISM

In working on the design for the NKTP sanatorium in Kislovodsk we tried at least to some extent to realize a socialist realist style. Our aim was to create the architectural form of a s a n a t o r i u m, in its c h a r a c t e r i s t i c, t y p i c a l t r a i t s — moreover, the form of a socialist sanatorium, i.e. of an institution which not only did not exist before, but also could not have come into existence during other historical epochs or under a capitalist society. Consequently, all the distinctive traits of this sanatorium need to be not architectural traits 'in general', but should stem as fully as possible, and as organically as possible, from the building's distinctive c o n t e n t.

For us, the first and most important stylistic trait of the socialist realist style was the embodiment in architecture of S t a l i n ' s g r e a t c a r e f o r h u m a n b e i n g s. It is this — and only this — which can help architects correctly draw up the brief, find the correct design for the building's organism, and pay constant attention to every little detail. The results of this can be seen in the southern orientation of all the sanatorium's residential rooms, in the attention paid to the treatment block, in the pains taken over providing comfort in the residential rooms, and so on.

Only an architect inspired by Stalin's care for people can take the right approach to a building's content in both its general features and details. Only in this way do architects find a reliable key to designing a site plan and determining a building's

spatial dimensions, thus determining the building's backbone, its true structure.

A no less important trait of socialist realism is sincerity and truthfulness of expression. A direct consequence of this is c o n f o r m i t y o f f o r m t o c o n t e n t. Without this condition, without an inextricable organic connection between form and content, socialist realism is impossible.

A detail or element only has to become form 'in general' — form which does not stem from and is not justified by content — for the architect to lose control of the steering wheel in his work, resulting sometimes in utterly random conclusions. For this reason, in the design of the main elements of the Kislovodsk sanatorium, we tried to listen as deeply as possible to the inner life of its organism and to reflect this life in architecture.

It was this internal life that defined the main concept for the sanatorium's master plan and all its characteristics. In just the same way the austere and self-contained shape of the treatment block arose from this building's internal structure.

The building's main horseshoe-shaped form, which contains a number of treatment rooms, does not require any special elements of external expression and thus remains simple and laconic. Only the main entrance, which should be welcoming and precise, compelled us to look for more complex means of expression. The large niche, which is slightly oriented towards those approaching it; the two columns clad in Byuk-Yankoy marble; the large glazed doorway

[27]

with the door: all these are devices which derive from the organic structure of the treatment block. On the other hand, for another part of the sanatorium — the rooms containing the Narzan baths — we resorted to looking for a new structure and decided on a circular block with an internal courtyard. The large recreational rooms made it possible to insert large loggias and glazed surfaces, rhythmically alternating with other elements, on the outside of the treatment block.

The open, extended character of the facades is, of course, determined by the structure of these residential blocks. In the main block, that part of the facade which contains the windows of the single rooms forms a continuous system of terraces; in the part which fronts the double rooms, loggias alternate rhythmically with windows. In block no. 2 there is a chequerboard pattern of windows and loggias on the wall surface. These architectural features stem from the character of the rooms whose windows punctuate this or that particular facade.

On the flat roofs of the residential blocks are trellises, flowerbeds, solaria and gardens. This significantly helps to bring out the specific character of the sanatorium, to link the architecture with the nature of the south.

We did our best, therefore, to find the sanatorium's principal architectural traits directly in the building's content. Does this mean that these elements of architecture were the only ones possible and were inevitable for this project? Of course not — because the creative process depended also on a number of subjective factors.

N e v e r t h e l e s s , i t s e e m s t o u s t h a t a m u l t i p l i c i t y o f o b j e c t i v e e l e m e n t s o f c o n t e n t h a v e b e e n c r y s t a l l i z e d h e r e i n f e a t u r e s w h i c h h a v e d e f i n e d t h e c h a r a c t e r i s t i c , t y p i c a l p a r t i c u l a r i - t i e s o f t h e S o v i e t s a n a t o r i u m . It was in following, as far as we could, the internal structure of the sanatorium, in developing the volumetric and spatial concept, that, in spite of all the mistakes and shortcomings, we endeavoured to arrive at a form that cannot be imparted to any other building.

A no less important trait of socialist realism, of course, is s i m p l i c i t y o f e x p r e s s i o n . However, this simplicity should have nothing in common with the meagreness of asceticism. What we were aiming at was that less easily attainable simplicity which should be inextricably bound up with profound elaboration of form, that simplicity which arises after a lengthy process of weeding out everything that is superfluous and unnecessary, where form

is crystallized in its most laconic and at the same time most profound and most striking expression.

It is very clear that we did not always attain this simplicity, or not always to the extent that we would have liked. Nevertheless, this was our constant ideal throughout the work, and the positive results which we managed to achieve, to a greater or lesser degree, should undoubtedly be ascribed to this clearly grasped aspiration.

Our view was that a simplicity of architectural elements should be linked to two architectural qualities — p l a s t i c i t y o f f o r m and o r g a n i c e x p r e s s i o n o f f o r m .

We tried to attain plasticity by means of a r i c h l y v a r i e d i n t e r p r e t a t i o n o f t h e e x t e r n a l w a l l a n d i n t e r p r e t a t i o n o f t h e f o r m i t s e l f . We realized the first objective through the specific character of the theme (a series of colonnades, loggias and balconies), which made it possible to achieve spatial depth by varying the external wall. We approached the problem of the plasticity of the form itself with considerably greater timidity and diffidence. The reason for this was our desire to avoid the danger of employing techniques in the plastic treatment of form that have been uncritically adopted from a particular historical style.

While we believe it is necessary to learn persistently and intensively from the best examples of our heritage, we are nevertheless firmly convinced that socialist realism — the style of our great age — should find its own special, distinctive plastic language which is peculiar to it alone. For this reason we tried to find a plastic expression of form which would resound in as contemporary a way as possible.

This is seen in the design of the crowning cornice; the profiling of particular horizontal or vertical articulations; the interpretation of the support not as a pillar but as a plastic element; the profiled edging of the loggias; and the shapes of the vases and other details. We tried to make all these elements as simple as possible; we introduced this or that articulation or string course only as the result of a clearly understood need for their use as plastic or organic expression of what is essentially a structural element. We are entirely satisfied with the principle and method of working that we adopted, as with the experience we acquired on this path. However, the specific results of this method were in many cases unsuccessful. By no means in all cases did we find the right scale for particular articulations; too many profiles are crude and primitive. In spite of the utter clarity of the task confronting us, its realization involved innumerable hidden difficulties.

50. Detail from the terracotta panel by the sculptor Zelensky in the niche of the restraining wall of the treatment block

Another aspect of the same problem was the need to find an o r g a n i c a p p r o a c h to form, because form becomes truly plastic when it has an organic structure. The first principle of organicity is, in our opinion, that the form should possess a clearly expressed beginning and end, bottom and top, and clear limits and boundaries of the organism. For this reason all the sanatorium's blocks have a clearly expressed bottom and top and a lightening of the form from bottom to top.

The bottom storeys of all the blocks are heavy and monumental; clad in dolomite, they rest firmly on the ground. All the blocks are topped by trellises and light roofs which create a grid of lines that almost dissolve in the air.

Another characteristic of an organic design is that the building's architectural articulations should simultaneously be structural articulations of the organism itself. Thus we avoided purely decorative articulations such as string courses and pilasters. Only in those places where there is an organic need for a functional division into struc-

tural parts or for elements to perform load-bearing work did we introduce architectural articulations; moreover, the nature of the interpretation was dictated by the articulations' purely tectonic role. Finally, specific articulations occur in places where two different elements, two different materials or two different systems come into contact or join together. For instance, if you have a plastered wall surface and perpendicular to it a dolomite-clad surface of a loggia, there is an organic need for some kind of articulation, edging or profiling at this intersection. Or again, if you have a ground storey clad in dolomite coming into contact with a plastered upper storey in one and the same plane, some kind of string course is required at the point where the intersection occurs. The same goes for cornices at the top of buildings and cornices which provide protection from rainfall.

A particular problem we experienced concerned the parts of a column. The intersection of the vertical support and the horizontal beams at the top and bottom leads, by analogy with the other examples,

[29]

to the need for structural articulations of some kind, performing the roles of base and capital.

Think of any historical epoch and you will see the importance of the role played by the classical order in forming the style of that epoch. The order was especially important in Greek architecture, where the peripter, as the main expression of the organism of Greek building types, was interpreted with infinite subtlety and profundity in the form of the two most typical orders — the Doric and Ionic. If we omit this idea from the history of Hellenist architecture, the very meaning of this great art, the most plastic and organic of all historical styles, will to a very large extent be lost.

But at the same time architectural analysis and in-depth study of the history of architecture shows us how the classical order in its specific expression may be inextricably bound up with the particularities of a style in general; it is therefore entirely possible that when the order of a particular historical style is copied in Soviet architecture, undesirable consequences may follow.

We tried various means to address this extremely complex problem in the buildings of the Kislovodsk sanatorium. In the external colonnades we introduced barely detectable structural changes, such as a simple slab at the bottom, and at the top a slight widening — a flower-like unfolding that serves as a transition to the upper slab.

In the internal orders, in the interiors of the blocks, we attempted to find a solution for the top of the column; these attempts involved the idea of an improved transition to the architrave. Here we also resorted to using different colours of paint.

It has to be admitted that the results of most of these ideas were not entirely satisfactory. Almost all the design solutions, with a few exceptions, merely pose the problem, but do not solve it. To find a definitive solution, a considerable period of time and numerous different attempts and experiments will be needed.

In our view, the socialist realist style, for all its simplicity, is inextricably bound up with enormous joie de vivre, verve and relevance in its expression. Above all, this may be attained by synthesizing architecture with other forms of art, i.e. with painting and sculpture. When simple geometrical architectural forms are placed alongside painting or sculpture, in other words when abstract architectural forms are juxtaposed with the human body and natural phenomena — the content of painting and sculpture — the contrast reveals and deepens the impact of each of these arts, infinitely enriching the impression that they make.

However, this can only happen when there is a real kinship between the different art forms, when the work of architecture and the work of painting or sculpture are infused with the same single ideological striving, derive from the same style, and have arisen from the synthetic execution of a single spatial task. Often in our practice a sculpture or picture fills a 'vacant spot', serving as a kind of ornament or merely a decorative flourish. This kind of approach, of course, has nothing to do with synthesis.

During the course of our work we tried to solve this difficult problem. Moreover, right from the start of work on designing the sanatorium, we tried to resolve numerous general problems of a spatial character through collaboration between our architects and the painters Rublev, Prussakov and the team led by Favorsky, and the sculptors Zelensky and Sotnikov. Unfortunately, so far we have only been able to implement a small part of our original ideas, although more has been achieved in the detailed designs and models. For instance, all the main interiors in the treatment block — the entrance hall and courtyard with the Narzan baths — were conceived together with the artist Rublev, while the dining room in the block was conceived with the team of artists led by Bruni and Favorsky. The panel in the entrance hall, which is painted on gesso, is organically linked with the white marble of the walls and the overall spatial design of the room. Especially important is the artists' work in the spatial design of the Narzan courtyard, where the white-faience frieze with doves above a wall of continuous glass is one of the most important parts of the overall spatial concept. Similarly, a large bas relief of coloured faience by the sculptor Zelensky is to be installed on the axis of the treatment block, in the retaining wall between the staircases. Without this bas relief the compositional axis would be incomplete and the overall concept greatly reduced in terms of its incisiveness and expressiveness.

In the overall look of the sanatorium, the fountains, pools, summerhouses, ramps, paths and other elements of minor and garden-and-park architecture play an extremely important role. However much we tried to attain a maximal s y n t h e s i s o f a r c h i t e c t u r a l f o r m s a n d s u r r o u n d i n g n a t u r e, the contrast between the abstract geometrical forms of the architecture and the infinitely mutable, plastic matter of nature has not been overcome. What is needed is the introduction of intermediate forms which do not destroy the compositional significance of the contrast, but soften its abruptness. Our idea is that this role should be performed by these elements of minor architecture and garden and park architecture.

In this way the staircase situated on the main axis of the entire composition is also extremely significant — something we realized at the very beginning of our design work. Given the slightly awkward angle made by the planes of the residential and treatment blocks, and given the need to find a transition in the terrain of the cliffs between the area at the top and the park at the bottom, the staircase was not a 'minor' architectural form, but an extremely important compositional link for the entire arrangement of buildings. Over the course of one and a half years we made numerous sketches and models of various versions of staircases; none of them were good enough. Finally, we arrived at the idea of using the location's natural terrain — i.e. of building a staircase in the form of an amphitheatre. Although this design, too, had its flaws, the staircase has made the composition of the sanatorium stronger and more coherent.

The amphitheatre has ensured an organic linking of the upper area with the lower, reconciling the cliffs of the precipice with the gentle contours of the valley bottom; it has reinforced the central role of the treatment block in the composition, serving as an excellent base for this block; and, most importantly, it has convincingly linked together the planes of the facades of the residential blocks with the facade of the treatment block.

I have already pointed out deficiencies in the design for the sanatorium which have affected particular parts and details of the structure. Many of the mouldings and elements of the decoration have turned out to be not entirely in proportion. Some of the cornices, for instance, are too large; others are too small. Some are excessively articulated; others are lacking in articulation. Many parts of the supports are unsatisfactory. The problem of the detail — proportionate detail — remains an extremely

difficult one for Soviet architecture; to resolve it considerable practical experience is required. In order to guess the correct scale of a detail situated 10—15 metres or more from the ground, you need intuition and considerable experience.

But an even more serious defect can be seen in the design for the Kislovodsk sanatorium: an insufficient clarity and precision in the overall compositional shape of the main blocks.

It became very clear to us that the overall composition of the structure may be highly complex, and the design of the articulations and details of each building extremely rich, diverse and proportional, but its overall outline and spatial dimensions should be as simple and understated as possible.

This is what we learn not just from the mistakes in this building, but from the entire experience of world architecture, and especially from Hellenist architecture, which attained a maximal compositional complexity, a maximal subtlety, and a maximal plasticity and proportionality of its buildings, while retaining a laconic and simple outline for the buildings. In the sanatorium building the main mistake is that the shape of the main block is too fussy, its outline insufficiently understated. And whereas on the south side this is not so immediately visible, on the north side all the flaws in the volumetric and spatial design of the main block are self-evident.

The comments made by the many delegations and tour groups who have visited the sanatorium are a sign that, in spite of its considerable flaws, the architecture of the sanatorium also contains numerous merits which users cannot but notice. What has been achieved here should be attributed entirely to the close-knit team of architects, artists, engineers, builders and doctors, led by the amazing architect and people's commissar comrade Sergo Ordzhonikidze (now deceased) and united and guided, above all, by Stalin's care for the people.

CONSTRUCTION. ORGANIZATION OF ENGINEERING

GENERAL PREMISES

The design organizing body was faced with a series of complex and important tasks. From the very beginning of work on the project, it took the approach of tackling all issues relating to architecture and construction, as well as special issues relating to equipment, in a coherent fashion. Only in this way was it possible to ensure the detailed design of the project as a whole, and of all its individual parts, in a way that satisfied the brief, and to ensure the best use of all the technical possibilities available today.

Close collaboration between specialists with various qualifications ensured an organic fusion of architecture and engineering art in the project.

The design work was carried out by round-the-clock multidisciplinary teams led by the organizing body which was responsible for the project as a whole. Overall management of the entire project was carried out by Architectural and Design Workshop No. 3 at the People's Commissariat for Heavy Industry; the design of sanitary and technical projects was carried out by Vodokanalproekt and Santekhproekt; the electrical-supply projects were drawn up by Stroyelektro; and so forth.

Finding solutions to the design and construction of large sanatorium complexes makes substantial demands on engineering and technical skills. In the case of this project, the complexity of the engineering tasks was exacerbated by higher-than-usual quality requirements. Before starting the design work, the authors of the project had to comprehensively study key aspects of the techno-logical process and the best way in which to organize the medical and health provision.

The sanatorium's technical infrastructure is based on the latest advances in construction, as well as balneological and sanitary/hygienic, technology.

In working on particular types of equipment or particular elements of equipment, the designers started by comprehensively studying the current state of the given sector of technology.

Admittedly, in numerous cases, it proved impossible to avoid mistakes; many types of equipment are still by no means free of flaws.

Some sectors of the industry in construction parts had to be restructured to meet what was required of them; this involved expanding the ranges of items they manufactured.

For sanatoria one of the main issues is the sanitary/technical and special equipment. Water supply plays a substantial role in matters of hygiene and therapy (hydrotherapy and so on). A practical design for the heating and energy infrastructure is instrumental in ensuring that the sanatorium can function without interruption.

All these issues had a direct impact on the overall organization of the site (the layout of the roads, the planning of the drains, the organization of the terrain, and so on).

Systematic, coherent design work also facilitated better organization of the installation and construction works.

Linking the timing of the general construction work with the sanitary-technical work made it possible to

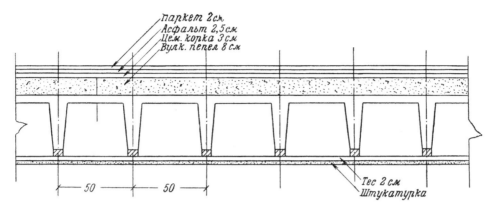

51. One of the types of floor/ceiling structure

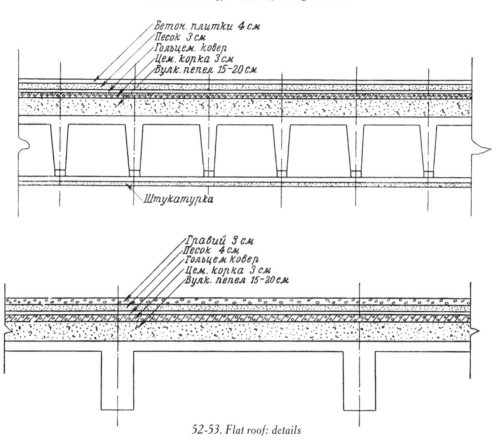

52-53. Flat roof: details

take into account the main installation requirements that apply in the execution of construction work (channels, ducts, niches, access hatches, apertures, and so on).

All this made it possible to improve the quality of the fit out. Additional works and alterations relating to laying sanitary/technical and special systems were kept to a minimum.

CHOICE OF MAIN CONSTRUCTION MATERIALS

In selecting construction materials for the sanatorium the designers based their choice on the desire to ensure that the buildings were monolithic and strong enough to last for many years. All the load-bearing structures are of brick and reinforced concrete;

secondary structures are of other materials that satisfy the given requirements.

To insulate the ceiling/floor structures and thermally insulate the flat roofs, a local material was used — volcanic ash. This volcanic ash, consisting

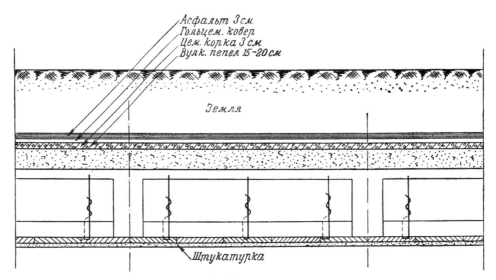

54. Flat roof: details

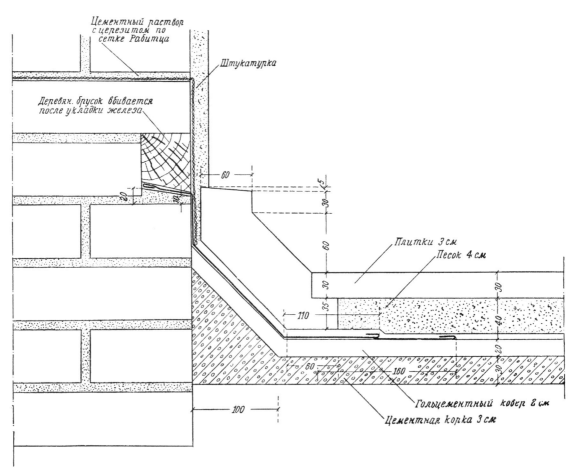

55. Flat roofs: details

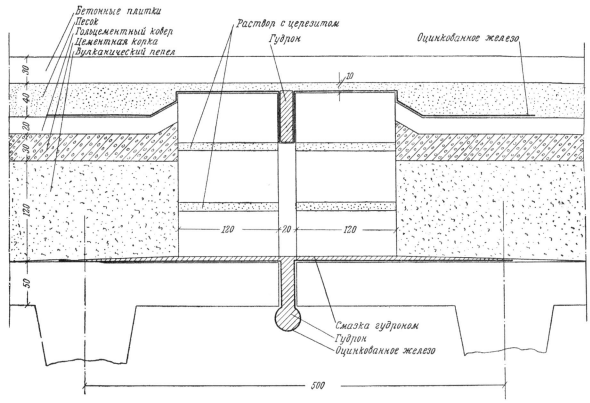

Бетонные плитки
Песок
Гольцементный ковер
Цементная корка
Вулканический пепел

Раствор с церезитом
Гудрон

Оцинкованное железо

10

80
40
20
30
120
50

120   20   120

500

Смазка гудроном
Гудрон
Оцинкованное железо

56. Flat roofs: details

of porous particles up to 4 mm in size, is fire-resistant, easily compacted, and a poor conductor of sound. It also has a low density.

For the external cladding extensive use was made of a local stone — dolomite. This is a limestone which has taken on a warm shade of light yellow, with a temporary resistance to compression of $280-350 \ \text{kg/cm}^2$.

Dolomite is easily worked using steel instruments (chisels, tooth axes, claw chisels, toothed chisels). It was used both for cladding the facades of entire buildings (the treatment block) and for parts of the facades.

For the external cladding use was also made of grey sandstone (the garage, the administrative block, the retaining walls), travertine and trachyte.

The external steps of the staircases are mainly of granite.

For internal cladding of the walls use was made of marble from the Urals, Crimea and Transcaucasia (Tagil, Koelga, Ufaley, Byuk-Yankoy, Shrosha, Sadakhlo).

The cabinetry work in the main blocks is of hardwoods such as oak, walnut, sycamore and beech, and in the service buildings and administrative block it is of pine.

CEILING/FLOOR STRUCTURES

A building's ceiling/floor structures usually have to satisfy requirements of strength, resistance to fire, and economy. In addition to these main requirements, in the case of sanatoria ceiling/floor structures are faced with stricter requirements concerning sound insulation. As is well known, complete sound insulation of ceiling/floor structures is for the moment unattainable in mass construction. In the types of ceiling/floor structure currently in use sound waves are transmitted through elements which are firmly joined to one

another. This is additionally made possible by the fact that in most cases the layer of insulation is situated between the load-bearing beams, without covering them. For this reason all the ceiling/floor structures in the main blocks in the NKTP sanatorium have a continuous layer of sound insulation uninterrupted by beams, joists, partition walls, or other elements. The insulation layer of volcanic ash is 10—12 cm thick.

A 2—2.5 cm layer of asphalt makes the ceiling/floor structures impermeable to water and air.

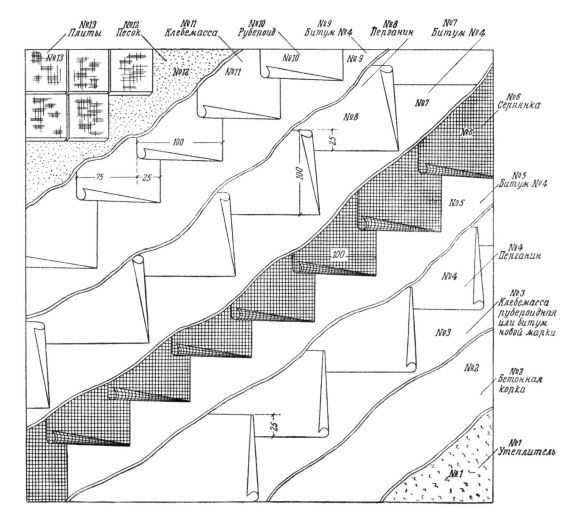

57. Flat roof: details

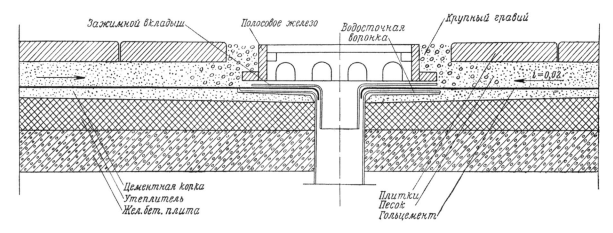

58. Rainwater heads

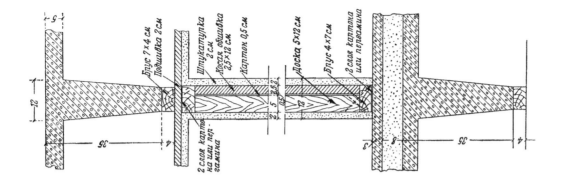

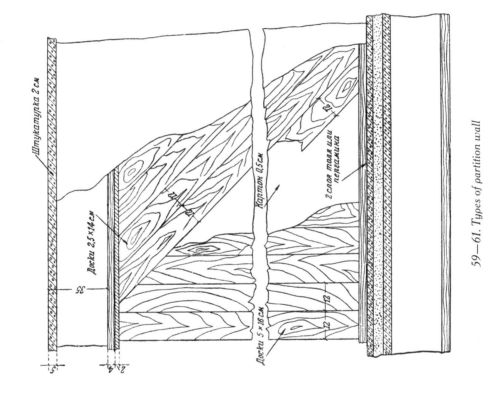

59—61. Types of partition wall

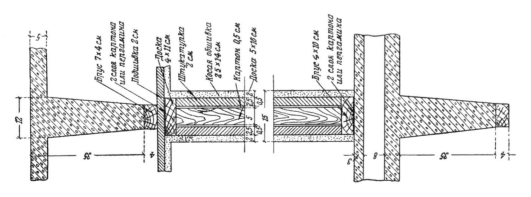

[37]

The diversity of types of floor/ceiling structure used can be linked to the diversity of architectural solutions and the specific functions of the buildings and rooms.

The different types of ceiling/floor structure differ only in terms of their sheathing material. It has to be noted that sheathing costs less than other methods and saves on metal, which is in short supply. In addition, wooden sheathing makes for faster execution of plasterwork because it enables the use of cement made from lime and alabaster. Plastering using Rabitz mesh is only possible when cement mortar, or a cement mortar with small admixtures of lime, is used. This kind of plaster takes much longer to dry than plaster based on lime and alabaster, since cement mortar is much slower to set when it is applied.

The most rational and cost-saving ceiling/floor structures are reinforced-concrete structures with small ribs (see Fig. 51). The saving of concrete and iron in ceiling/floor structures with small ribs is inconsiderable compared to the savings which may be attained using ordinary ribbed structures. But the cost of the formwork is considerably reduced due to the possibility of using standard formwork for all the floor/ceiling structures. Boxes of two to three types (middle and end boxes) which have been made for one section can be used for all the others too. The prefabricated boxes make it possible to assemble the formwork for the ceiling/floor structure with great rapidity. The tilted edges of the ribs make the dismantling of this formwork also quick and problem-free. The formwork could be used up to 25 times, which significantly reduced the cost of the reinforced-concrete work.

The type of ceiling/floor structure used here also has structural advantages. The sheathing for creating a smooth ceiling can very conveniently be fastened to the blocks of wood which are left on the lower edges of the ribs following removal of the formwork boxes. This kind of ceiling/floor structure also provides the best soundproofing.

FLAT ROOFS

All the buildings in the sanatorium complex have flat roofs. These may be divided into two types — usable roofs and non-usable ones. The difference between the two types is a matter of their outer covering, of the degree to which the covering abuts the vertical surfaces of the parapets, and of how the expansion joints are arranged.

As can be seen from figures 52 and 53, the reinforced-concrete slab is thermally insulated by a layer of volcanic ash. A cement mortar screed is laid on top of the compacted layer of ash. The top surfaces of the insulation layer and the cement screed are tilted towards the rainwater heads.

The wood-cement carpet which is glued to the cement screed is protected from mechanical impacts by concrete slabs which are 4 cm thick and are laid on a 3 cm layer of sand.

The concrete slabs (of terrazzo) were poured on site along strips which had been laid in advance in special patterns. After the concrete had set, the strips were removed, and the resulting 4–5 cm wide seams were filled with nutritive earth. Planted with seeds of trample-resistant grass, these seams form a green grid.

The roof of block no. 2 was intended for the creation of a small garden consisting of dwarf bushes and trees. Planting these bushes and trees required a considerable layer of earth. To protect the wood-cement carpet from the destructive impact of the roots of bushes and trees, a 3 cm protective layer of asphalt was laid on the roof. To prevent rainwater being retained for too long before descending, a drainage system consisting of wooden boxes was created in the layer of earth.

In the non-usable roofs a 4–5 cm layer of gravel was used instead of concrete slabs to serve as protection.

The most vulnerable spot in a flat roof is where it abuts vertical surfaces. These areas of abutment were designed as shown in Fig. 55. When it came to it, however, the manufacture of border stones had not been set up in time, so the plastering was extended up to the roof slabs. But the plastering in the bottom part was very quick to crack and turn to dust (during the course of a single season). The reason for this was insufficient cohesion between the thin layer of plaster (on the Rabitz mesh) and the apron of zinced metal.

In order to screen off the vertical parts of the roof, reliable protection was created in the form of a brick wall stretching up to the cornice.

The expansion and settlement joints were designed to have two compensators of galvanized steel or sheet lead (Fig. 56). However, being made of galvanized steel, they started leaking above the treatment block, especially in the spots where the roof abutted the parapet.

This happened due to the fact that insufficient care had been taken in soldering the seams and as a result of difficulties relating to execution of the curved part of the compensator of galvanized steel.

The latter circumstance compelled us to make the compensators from sheet lead. These have proved entirely reliable.

The construction of the wood-cement carpet (Fig. 57) is of interest. Its strength was considerably enhanced by introducing an additional layer of calico.

The reasons why sheet roofing leaks may be divided into two main categories: 1) a failure to comply with the technical conditions for construction of such roofs (roofing materials with defects; unsatisfactory base; and so on), and 2) mechanical damage.

Cases in the latter category are the more frequent. Even when painstaking preventative measures are taken during the construction of roll-based roofs (working in soft footwear etc.), there is no guarantee that the surface will remain intact: it is possible that mechanical damage can occur during the execution of subsequent works that require heavy materials to be transported over the roof (sprinkling sand, laying of concrete slabs or border stones, installation of railings, etc.).

When work is done on a flat roof, uneven pressure is brought to bear on various parts of the roof — by the barrow runs, boxes with cement, various supports for heavy objects, and so on — due to the way the roof tilts.

In these cases an additional layer of calico becomes very important since it redistributes local pressures, transmitting them to larger areas.

Conditions at Kislovodsk make the elimination of rainwater from the flat roofs especially important, given the frequent downpours that occur during the rainy season (April to July). Water is removed by internal drainpipes situated in such a way that the path taken by the water from the most distant points to the drain itself does not exceed 12 metres.

The design of the drainpipe rainwater heads is shown in Fig. 58.

A drawback of this design is the reduction in the effective cross-section of the receiving rainwater head due to the gluing on of the top layers of wood-cement carpet.

The flat roofs on the buildings passed all the tests to which they were subjected with flying colours, and their use presents no problems.

It should once again be underlined that the reliability of a flat roof depends mainly on the correct organization of the building work.

PARTITION WALLS

In addition to the usual requirements applying to partition walls, in the construction of sanatoria it is particularly important to ensure requirements concerning sound insulation and compliance with sanitary/hygienic conditions.

The partition walls in our sanatorium were designed in such a way as to be capable of containing concealed pipes for sanitary and technical devices.

There are four types of partition wall in terms of function.

Partition walls of the first type divide residential rooms. The expedience of using discards from formwork, scaffolding and cabinetry work determined the choice of material for these partitions, which are multilayered and made of planks (Figs. 59–61).

In this design the middle supporting boards rest not directly on the structure but on a springy lining made from cardboard.

Between the partition wall and the load-bearing walls there is also a springy lining. The partition is fastened to the load-bearing walls using ordinary fasteners. On both sides of the middle board a single layer of cardboard is laid for the purpose of sound insulation. For the planked battens, use is made only of dry discards which have been carefully selected.

The way these partition walls are built rules out the possibility of cracks appearing right the way through

a wall, while the absence of empty spaces within the wall makes it difficult for rodents to multiply.

The second type of partition wall divides residential rooms in the double unit or separates residential rooms from individual entrance areas.

These walls are built in the same way as partitions of the first type, but with the difference that there are fewer layers of wood.

Since these partition walls divide spaces which are usually used by just one person, the requirements concerning sound insulation are in this case less stringent than those applying to the first type of partition.

The third type of partition is used in rooms where there is a constant source of moisture (bathrooms, shower rooms, rooms for treatments involving moisture, and so on). Inside these partition walls special channels contain concealed pipes carrying hot and cold water, sewage, etc.

On the side facing the corridor the channels in the partition walls in toilets and bathrooms in the first residential block have 2-metre-high apertures fronted by panels. Opposite the apertures for inspecting the pipes, easily removable sections have been incorporated in the panels.

The partition walls in the main block have the same constructional design, but here the sections opposite the apertures are hinged.

These 8- and 6-cm thick partitions with a lining of single mesh are made from concrete.

In order to reduce acoustic permeability, volcanic ash and brick chips were used as the solid element in the concrete.

The identical dimensions of the bathroom units made it possible to use formwork that could be dismantled and re-used; the partitions were poured on site.

The fourth type of partition wall is an ordinary reinforced-concrete partition built in accordance with the function of the room.

The latter partitions were used mainly in buildings with a service function.

ORGANIZATION OF CONSTRUCTION WORK

The Georgievskoe Plateau on which the sanatorium was built is fringed by gullies to the north, west and south.

At the start of construction it was possible to drive onto the plateau only from the direction of Budennovka along an unpaved road. During the rainy season this road became impassable, which made it considerably more difficult to transport materials and to organize construction work.

The construction work was entrusted to Industroy, a powerful building organization which is part of Glavstroyprom NKTP.

Development of the site began with a study of the geological strata, their stability, and the behaviour of the groundwater.

A timetable for works to be carried out was drawn up based on the technical construction plans. The most urgent measure was to build the roads to be used by vehicles driving onto the building site. For this reason the first structure to be built was the main road connecting the city of Kislovodsk with the site.

Three storehouses for construction materials were set up. The first (for bulky and loose materials) was in the immediate vicinity of Kislovodsk freight station. The second storehouse was at the foot of the Georgievskoe Plateau from the direction of Budennovka. The third — the main storehouse — was on the western side of the plateau (in a location not intended for development).

A temporary garage was built for vehicles; this included workshops, storage for spare parts, and a depot for fuel.

To accommodate the workers, standard barracks buildings were erected on the top area in a spot relatively distant from the buildings, and on Shirokaya street in Budennovka. A barracks building was also erected for administrative and technical staff and, additionally, two houses were rented. On the top site a canteen was constructed for the builders.

Furthermore, quarries were established to supply stone, dolomite, sand and gravel. A mechanized carpentry shop and engineering and mechanical workshops were also set up.

The main difficulties were the lack of water and electric energy since the city's utilities infrastructure was unable to supply the construction site with these utilities.

In order to supply water, special reservoirs were built and filled at night through a connection with the city's pipe system. In order to supply electric energy, a diesel substation was built with a compressor for supplying the construction project with compressed air.

All structures to be built were split into three construction areas functioning as individual economic units.

The technical construction department was given responsibility for studying the quality of materials, overseeing a field laboratory for work involving concrete, observing how production processes were being carried out, and compiling technical documentation. Following execution, works were inspected and assessed by a special supervisory construction department which included members of the design organization body.

The plan for organization of works was partly altered and expanded on the construction site itself. Certain types of works were carried out as follows in accordance with the plan:

1. E a r t h - m o v i n g w o r k s. The volume of earthworks was up to 350,000 m³. Before the beginning of the main work on creating the layout for the site, the upper layer of black earth was removed and set aside. Subsequently, this earth was used when greenery was planted on the site.

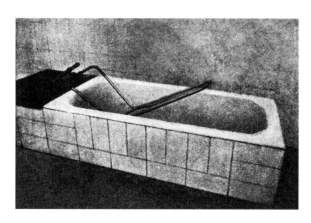

62. The Narzan baths are fitted with heated coils

63. Decorative radiator screen

The main earth-moving works related to building roads and levelling land on which buildings were to be erected.

First of all, underground works were carried out for utilities systems (water pipes, heating systems). This significantly speeded up construction of the main structures.

The hardest soils were dealt with mechanically. A substantial part of the earth-moving works was carried out using explosions and jack-hammers.

2. Stone, concrete, and reinforced-concrete works. Jib cranes and hoist towers were set up on the construction site.

Manufacture of concrete and cements was mechanized. The number of concrete mixers at each construction site was adjusted to suit current needs since they could be assembled and dismantled very quickly.

Materials raised by hoist were carried over the floors in barrows. Use was made of vibrating equipment during the pouring of the concrete.

The composition of the concrete for each new lot of materials (cement and stone materials) was determined depending on the planned grade. As concreting work was being carried out, a sample of the concrete was handed over to the field laboratory to be tested. The formwork was removed only after these samples had been tested. A special journal of concrete works was kept.

Stationary and moveable formwork was made at a special formwork yard.

Rebars were made at each construction site. To cut the rebars, use was made of lever scissors and a hand-operated press. In order to bend the rebars, workbenches with hand presses were installed.

Rebars with a diameter of more than 12 mm were joined together by electric welding.

3. Metal structures. All the metal structures (columns, beams, transoms, railings, and so on) were made at special mechanized workshops.

4. Carpentry work. A centralized carpentry workshop made the window transoms, doors, hardwood panels and cupboards for living rooms in the sanatorium. In addition, the carpentry workshop made various aids and wooden instruments — for instance, rules, templates, movable staircases, formwork, and so on.

Works in the carpentry workshop were mechanized. Items made at the carpentry workshop were assembled mainly on site.

* * *

The team of builders worked non-stop to master Stakhanovite methods of organizing labour.

64. Decorative radiator screen

[41]

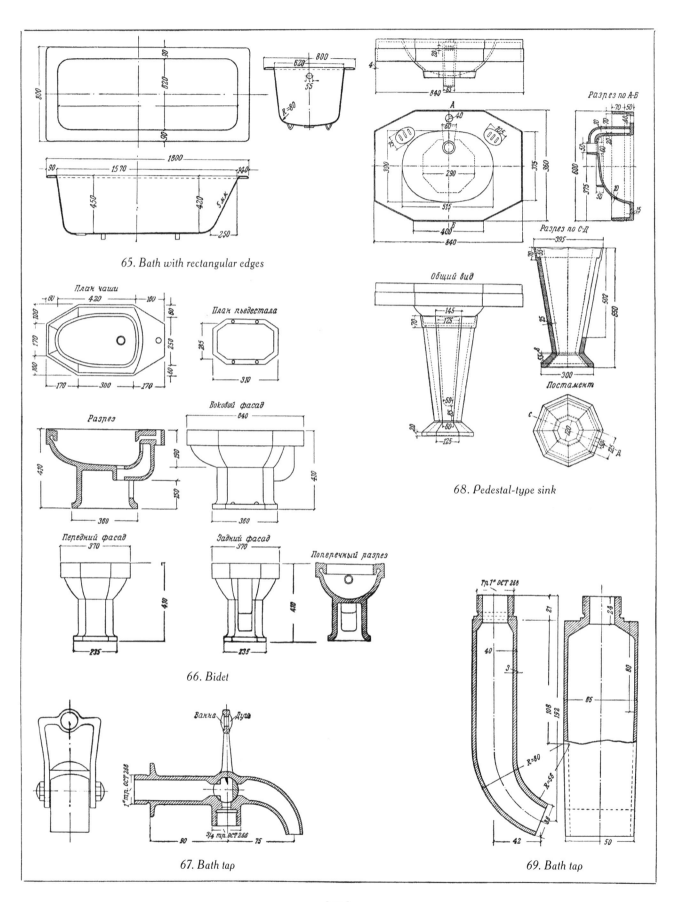

65. Bath with rectangular edges

66. Bidet

67. Bath tap

68. Pedestal-type sink

69. Bath tap

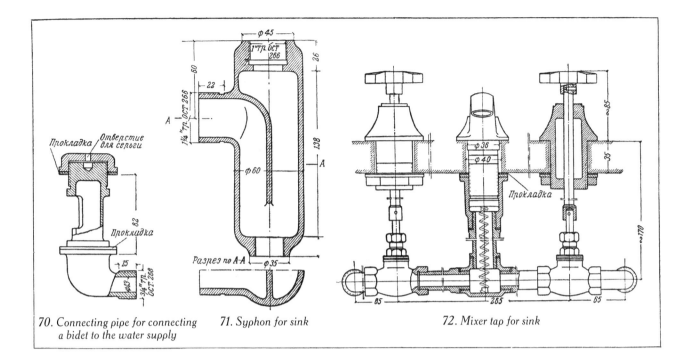

70. Connecting pipe for connecting
a bidet to the water supply

71. Syphon for sink

72. Mixer tap for sink

The entire team focused continuously on the following: ensuring that individual teams were supplied with materials in good time; the division of production processes between qualified and subsidiary workers; the rational installation of materials; the expedient placing of devices and mechanisms; and other issues concerning the most effective way to organize the workplace.

The number of Stakhanovites was sometimes as high as 90% of the total number of workers employed at the construction site.

The direct involvement of the designers/architects and engineers in the execution of construction works had a positive effect on the progress and quality of the work.

N.D. VISHNEVSKY

ISSUES RELATING TO EQUIPPING,
AND SUPPLYING UTILITIES TO, THE SITE

In establishing utilities on the site on which the sanatorium buildings were erected, the focus was on road-building and levelling the construction site.

Plans for levelling the site were drawn up by architects and engineers working together. This method proved very productive.

The layout of the roads was determined by the specific character of the site's terrain. All the roads have features which are typical of roads of a semi-mountainous type (tight bends, steep slopes, protective retaining walls, adjacent driveways situated on different levels, etc.).

One of the major engineering structures is the main driveway leading onto the sanatorium site on the north-west slope from the direction of the district of Budennovka.

An underground network of drainpipes (storm-water drainage) extends throughout the main area of the site.

Construction of the building housing the Narzan baths involved considerable difficulties since the site

is situated at a distance of 3 km from the spring from which the Narzan water comes. The difference in height between the Narzan spring and the sanatorium site is 180 metres. Initially, we intended to use two pumping stations with an intermediate substation to supply the Narzan; this would have ensured a normal pressure in the pipeline (for iron pipes about 10 atmospheres). The Narzan flows from Kislovodsk's municipal Narzan pumping station into a distributive reservoir situated near the sanatorium's treatment block. Thick-walled iron pipes intended to cope with a higher working pressure of 20 atmospheres (and tested under a pressure of 40 atmospheres) were made. It was decided to centralize the warming of the Narzan in special counterflow apparatuses before the water flows out into the baths.

The system of pipes for supplying water for drinking and housekeeping needs was equipped with a special device for softening the hard water (up to 36°) coming from the city's water pipe.

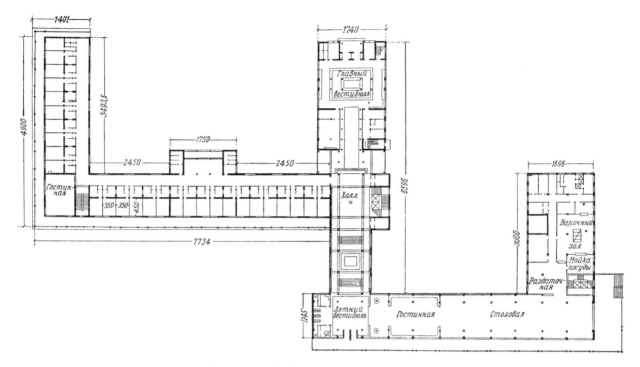

73. Dormitory block no. 1. Layout of the ground floor

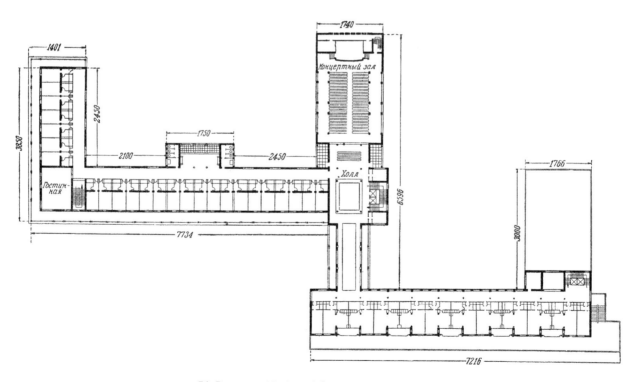

74. Dormitory block no. 1. Layout of the second floor

This device consists of two glauconite filters, a salt dissolver, a salt tank, a pump for breaking up the glauconite with salt water, a reservoir for the softened water, a pump to supply this water to the boilers, and a boiler.

Vertically, the sanatorium's network of pipes has numerous bends. For this reason, the design provides for special supports, casings, and so on.

The route taken by the sewage includes a considerable number of tumbling bays, supports, and other such special devices.

The location of the boiler-house in the services yard in the north-western part of the site is very successful: in views of the sanatorium seen from any point the boiler-house building stands at a distance from the sanatorium complex.

An underground concrete heating tunnel with a cross-section of 1800—2100 mm x 1200 mm was built in which to lay the main heating pipes.

Artificial lighting is an issue of considerable architectural significance since perception of architectural forms largely depends on lighting conditions.

The initial plan envisaged dividing the site into the following zones: a) mostly brightly illuminated areas (the top plateau with the main sanatorium blocks, the main parterre, the main entrance, and so on); b) less brightly illuminated areas (the alleys in the park, the main staircase, the summer-houses, and so on); c) areas with standard lighting (the services yard); and d) areas where the lighting is from special light sources (shaded, decorated or low-placed light sources: paths, grottos, and so on).

The grounds of the sanatorium are illuminated by spherical spotlights attached to masts.

Additionally, spotlights were installed on the pergolas of the main blocks.

ISSUES TO DO WITH SANITARY, TECHNICAL, AND SPECIAL EQUIPMENT IN CERTAIN BUILDINGS

During construction of the sanatorium, attention was focused on how to improve the general level of construction work, with extensive use being made of concealed pipes and utilities networks. Moreover, the quality of the equipment was improved — this was necessary to ensure that the various systems of pipes could function without fear of interruption.

When use was made of concealed pipes, it was necessary to avoid the pipes being covered up entirely, in order to allow them to be inspected during the construction process.

Concealed pipes are very good from the point of view of sanitation and hygiene; when pipes are left exposed, accumulations of dust are inevitable.

A number of options for the bathrooms were developed, but the choice fell on the so-called 'corridor type' of bathroom, where the bathroom directly abuts the residential room on one side and the corridor on the other (in block no. 2 and in the one-and-a-half-room units in block no. 1). Removable and openable decorative panels make it possible to inspect and repair

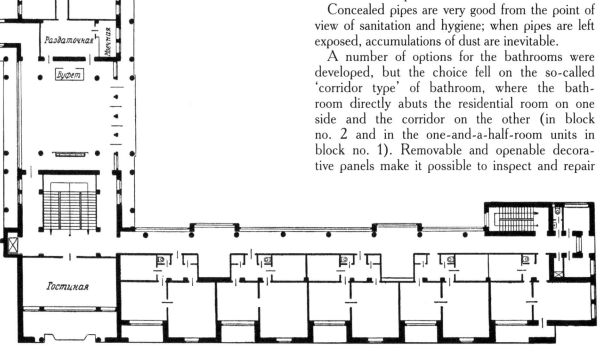

75. Dormitory block no. 2. Layout of the second floor

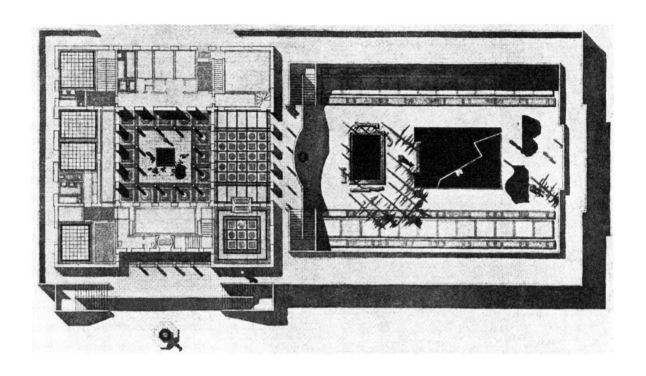

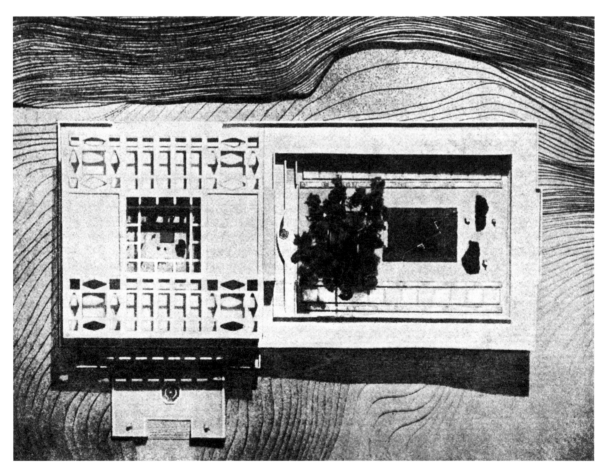

76. Block no. 3. General layout and view from above

[46]

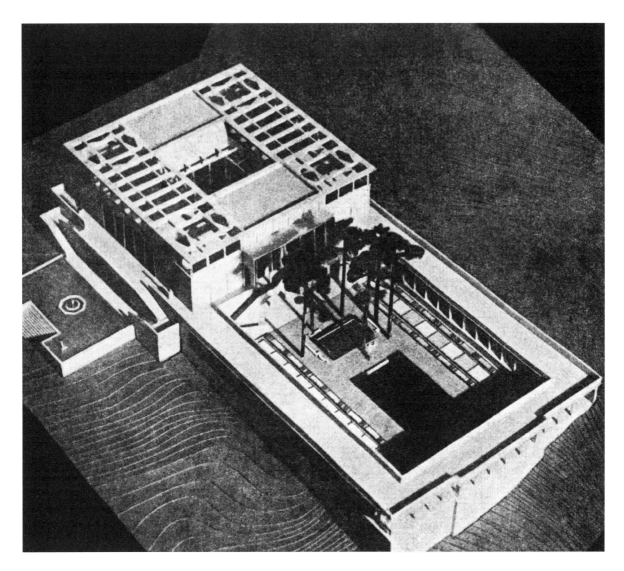

77. Block no. 3. Model

the pipes. This is the best way to acoustically insulate the residential rooms.

Considerable attention was paid to tying in the sanitary-technical and special works with the overall timetable for construction. The work was carried out by round-the-clock multidisciplinary teams.

The basement storey of the circular part of the treatment block contains an installation corridor. This gave rise to extraordinary advantages both in assembling the utilities networks and in observing their use. In general, such corridors simplify installation processes when there is a considerable concentration of special networks.

The vertical pipes and distributive network for the heating system in the main block and in block no. 2 were either assembled using concealed pipes

in special channels plastered over using Rabitz mesh or were screened off using panels, cupboards, and so on. The heating units in the main sanatorium blocks are decorated with special screens. The material of the screens (wood) makes it possible to eliminate defects in the operation of the heating devices with comparative ease.

The heating units in the bath building are installed in special concrete partition walls. The radiator has a metal grille, and there is a removable panel — allowing the unit to be observed in operation — on the side where the bathing cabin is situated.

In the main sanatorium blocks exhaust-ventilation ducts are concealed in installation cupboards mounted in the partitions. The bath building has supply-ventilation ducts installed in the columns.

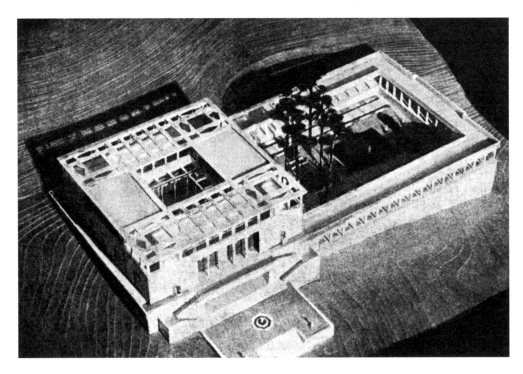

78–80. Block no. 3. Models

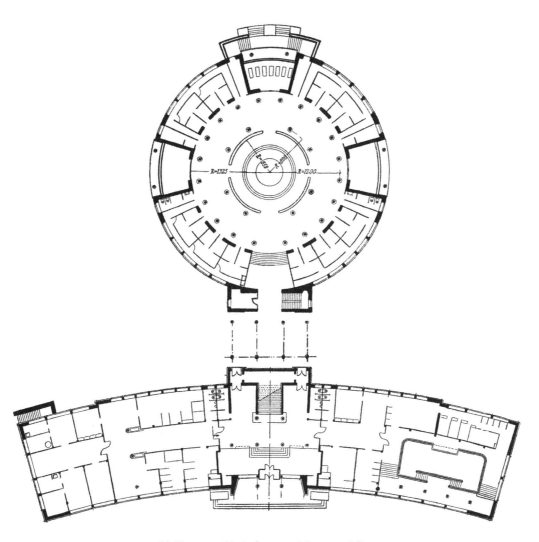

81. Treatment block. Layout of the ground floor

Throughout the sanatorium, ventilation devices are used as elements of interior architecture.

The exhaust-ventilation apertures are, as a rule, situated in the upper part of the rooms. Only in the cinema and the building with the Narzan baths (due to the settling of air saturated with carbon dioxide) are the exhaust-ventilation apertures situated at the bottom.

In many places the horizontal ventilation boxes are housed in a special casing.

The extensive use of flat roofs made the ventilation scheme more complex. Most of the exhaust-ventilation units had to be placed in the direct vicinity of the rooms being ventilated. TsAGI [Central Institute of Aerohydrodynamics] axial ventilators were used as the source of mechanical impulse for the exhaust-ventilation system. In order to dampen the noise, sound-insulation measures were taken (linings made from sound-absorbent materials, padding of walls and doors, etc.).

The air for the supply ventilation is taken from the green area; for ventilation units use is sometimes made of minor-form architecture (for instance, the pillar beside the treatment block).

The vertical water pipes in the main blocks are mounted in the partition walls of the bathrooms. The way these walls have been built allows pipe joins and fittings to be inspected. On the corridor side the pipe serving the bathrooms passes through the partition walls in special channels. It is decorated with removable and openable panels. In places the pipe is installed in a partition wall between two bathrooms; in these cases the removable panel is installed in one of the two bathrooms served by the pipe.

The fire-safety cupboards in the main blocks are likewise concealed behind panels.

The sewage downpipes and horizontal pipes removing wastewater from sanitary devices

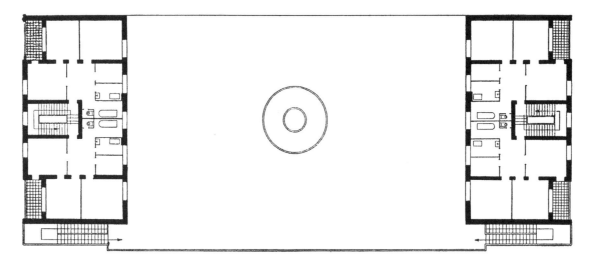

82. Layout of the second floor of the administrative block

in the main blocks are concealed in partition walls, floor/ceiling structures, and in special casings.

The doctors' reception rooms in the treatment block have downpipes situated in special channels which have been plastered over using Rabitz mesh.

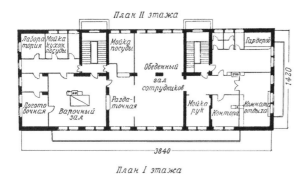

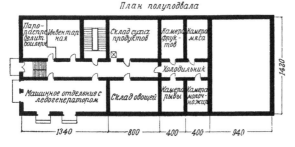

83. Layout of the dining room / food-preparation room

In the remaining buildings in the sanatorium and in ancillary rooms in the main blocks the sewage pipes have been left uncovered on top of the walls.

To take wastewater away from the hydro-treatment room there are special troughs covered with removable perforated panels. These are on the one hand used as waste-disposal channels; on the other, they contain pipes carrying cold and hot water.

The process of constant circulation of water in the pool occurs as follows: water flows in through a special cascade-type aperture in the middle part of the edge of the pool; the dirty layer of water on the surface flows off into a drain-off duct situated at the level of the water.

The positioning of the exhaust sewage pipes needed to avoid having a negative effect on how the flat roof was arranged and on the architectural/spatial perception of the buildings. For this reason, in the most important places the number of vertical ventilation pipes was kept to a minimum: we joined them together inside the building underneath the ceiling and tried to locate them in places which are least exposed to sight.

From a technical and architectural/artistic point of view, the internal removal of rainwater has indubitable advantages compared to its external removal.

The complete and rapid removal of water is achieved by the way the roof has been built — by the tilting of the roof and the judicious placing of rainwater heads. The way in which some of the roofs are used has affected the placing of the rainwater heads. Drainpipes passing through the inside of the building are concealed in partition walls.

For the internal illumination of the sanatorium's main blocks use has mainly been made of a special light fitting made to a design by the architecture workshop. The designers strove for good illumination (up to 75 lux in most rooms) which is adjustable within the required limits.

In some of the rooms artificial illumination was one of the principal aspects of the architectural organization of the interior (e.g. the luminous cornice in the cinema auditorium).

The wiring for the electrical network in the main blocks is concealed.

We placed particular importance on patients being able to summon the medical staff. To this end there is a special warning system: on the wards there are dual devices of a special design which patients can use to call a nurse or orderly, or both at the same time. When a button is pressed, lamps light up in the corridor above the doors (a red lamp for the orderly and a white lamp for the nurse); at the same time an alarm goes off in the duty room (a bell during the day and a buzzer during the night). The alarm is turned off only when the person summoned enters the room. The alarm may even be transferred to a room where the nurse or orderly is currently situated. In order to ensure the latter possibility, the member of staff must, after entering the room, insert a key into the sounder.

Patients can summon members of the administration (the ward sister, ward housekeeper, duty doctor, etc.) by phone through the duty officer at the telephone station, who turns on the search alarm. The latter comprises a system of dials situated in communal areas throughout the sanatorium. Each member of the sanatorium staff is given a particular number; when notified in this way, he or she contacts the duty officer at the telephone station so as to find out from the latter the place from which the call has come. There are also plans to create a fire-alarm system.

SANITARY DEVICES, LIGHTING AND SANITARY-TECHNICAL FITTINGS, SPECIAL DEVICES

The architecture workshop made a special effort to study modern types of sanitary devices. Given the state of this manufacturing sector, we had at our disposal, when we started construction work,

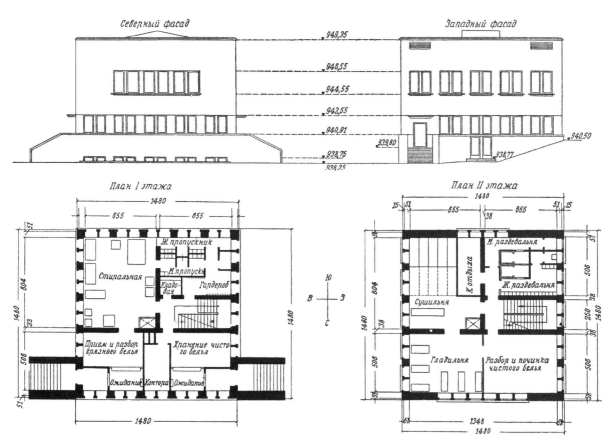

84. Layout of the laundry

only a dull and monotonous range of obsolete items of poor quality. We presented manufacturers of sanitary equipment with a series of requirements; our aim was to have pieces of equipment that are inexpensive, convenient, and of a fitting design.

The bathroom-equipment industry was asked to manufacture a number of items which had not yet been developed (syphon-type toilets, faience tanks, wash tables, bidets, baths with rectangular edges, special fittings, etc.). These orders were for the most part manufactured.

But the novelty of this issue for both designers and for the manufacturing factories had a negative effect on the quality of some of the items made.

The fact that these items were manufactured as part of a coherent programme ensured that the sanatorium was filled with items of equipment that were in harmony with one another. In addition, it made the processes of installation and assembly simpler.

Our work on the interior design of a room usually began by identifying the types of equipment it would contain. Thus we ensured the optimal architectural and spatial design of the interiors. There then came the need to position the equipment in harmonious conformity with the overall architectural design.

Each of the sanitary devices, in addition to satisfying its main function, had to be well designed. The sanitary/technical fittings had to be strong and elegant and at the same time simple and smooth.

For most sanitary appliances the optimal material is faience. Yet most of the faience items made at this time had notable defects (a yellow colour, dirty glazing, non-uniform firing, irregular shape, etc.). Many of the items that were needed (the bidet and so on) were altogether absent from manufacturers' catalogues. Special technical specifications had to be drawn up to cover the manufacture of these types of appliance.

Similar requirements were made of the metal-working industry. Specifically, it was necessary to ensure that the porcelain enamel used to coat the iron baths gave the baths the appearance of faience. All the sanitary appliances in the sanatorium are of a white colour. The faience WC set in the main blocks consists of a faience syphon toilet with a large low-positioned tank, also of faience. Made specially for the Moskva Hotel, this toilet is one of the most perfect types of equipment of its kind.

The washbasins are of two types: wash tables on legs (in the single rooms) and washbasins on pedestals (in the other residential rooms).

The bidets are of faience. The way they are made ensures that water is supplied at the required temperature through special apertures in the edge of the appliance.

All the sanitary appliances are located on the same wall.

The baths have a rectangular edge. Baths of this type do not have the defects that are characteristic of baths on legs — namely, the accumulation of dirt in spots which are inaccessible for cleaning, and water spilling underneath the bath.

The rectangular shape of the bath's edge made it easier to install in a special niche, and the facing of the bath's outer surface in marblite tiles ensured that it harmonizes with the overall decoration of the bathroom.

Installation of appliances of a superior type required sanitary/technical fittings of high quality. We did not scatter the fittings over the entire wall but, as far as possible, concentrated them in a single spot — very sensibly given that use was being made of concealed wiring: to gain access to the metal fittings, it is sufficient to remove a single tile. The necessity to supply hot water to almost all appliances required the installation of a large number of 'duplex' mixer taps.

The wash tables on legs are fitted with table-type fittings.

At the same time, particular types of fittings were made for the bidets, along with special parts for the sanitary appliances.

The electric-lighting fittings were used as an element in the architectural decoration of the rooms.

The single residential rooms are illuminated by a spherical pendant lamp with a 300-watt bulb, a spotlight (2 x 50 watts) suspended above the bed, a desk lamp, and a nightlight. The bathrooms are illuminated by a special ceiling lamp and a two-bulb horizontal spotlight. The double rooms are illuminated in the same way, except that here a spotlight has been added above the mirror, as well as a ceiling lamp in the entrance area and a spotlight in the toilet. The living rooms and restaurants are illuminated by chandeliers and standing lamps; the entrance halls, corridors, and passageways are lit by special ceiling lamps, standing lamps, and sconces. The ancillary and service buildings and rooms are fitted with standard types of light fitting.

Especially noteworthy among the individual sanitary and hygienic appliances is the special reinforced-concrete indoor swimming pool (rectangular in shape).

The pool's depth is 0.6 metres at its entrance and 1.3 metres at its lowest point.

A.I. SHNEYEROV

85. General view of the sanatorium

86. General view of the treatment block

87. General view of the treatment block from the south

89. The treatment block from the roof of dormitory block no. 1

88. View of the treatment block through the colonnade of dormitory block no. 1

90. The swimming pool

91. Part of the Narzan baths building

92. *The entrance hall of the treatment block*

95. *The Narzan baths room in the treatment block*

94. *The Narzan baths room in the treatment block*

96. The Narzan baths room in the treatment block

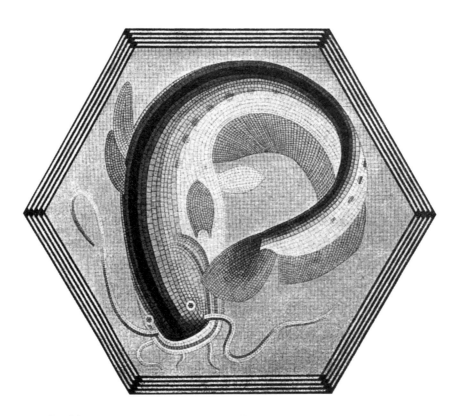

97—98. Marble mosaic in the floor of the Narzan baths room in the treatment block

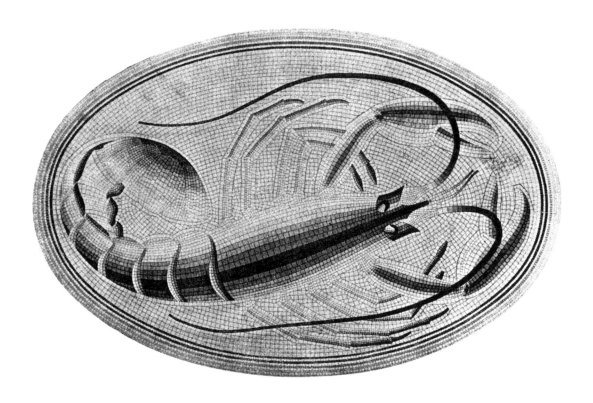

99–100. Marble mosaic in the floor of the Narzan baths room in the treatment block

101. The interior of the courtyard

102. Part of the restraining wall and the staircase of the treatment block

103. The main staircase in front of the treatment block

[63]

104. Part of the main staircase

105. Part of the main staircase

106. Part of the main staircase

107. Part of the main staircase

108. The main staircase and the ramp leading to the lower park

109. View of block no. 1 from the roof of block no. 2

110. General view of block no. 1 from the south

111. General view from the south

112. Part of the concert hall

114. Part of the block containing single rooms

113. Part of the block containing double rooms

115. General view of block no. 1 from the south

116–117. General view of block no. 1 from the south

118—119. The trellis on the roof of the concert hall

120. The trellis on the roof of the concert hall

121. The main entrance hall

122. The cinema and concert hall

123. The cinema and concert hall

124. Detail of the ceiling in the dining room

125. The ceiling in the living room

126. The corridor alongside the single rooms

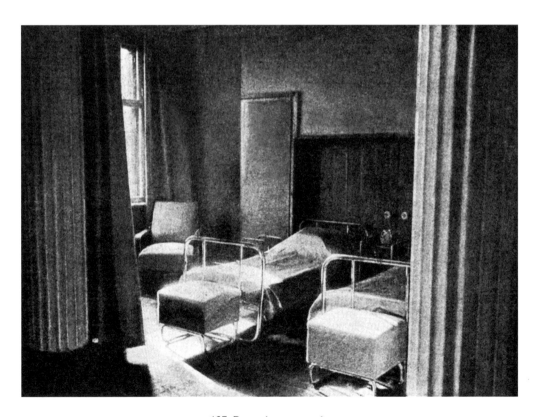

127. Room for two people

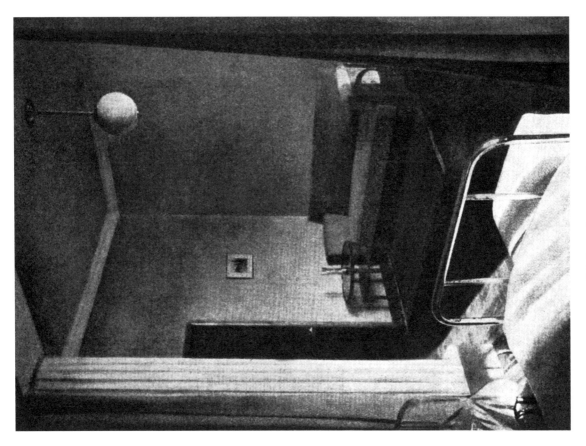

129. Room for two people

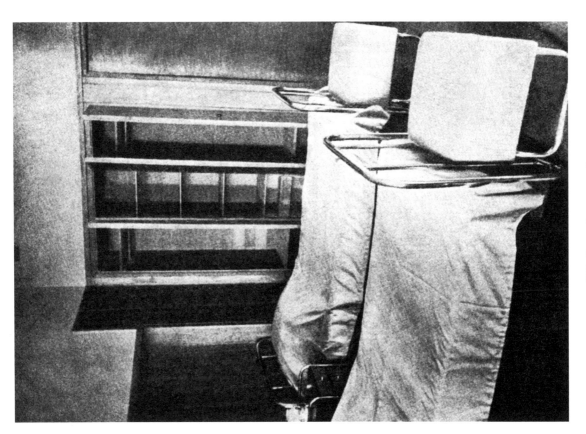

128. Room for two people

130. View of block no. 2 from the roof of block no. 1

131. General view of block no. 2 and the main staircase

[78]

133. *General view of block no. 2*

132. *General view of block no. 2*

134. Roof garden

135. Corridor

136. The winter garden

138. Corridor

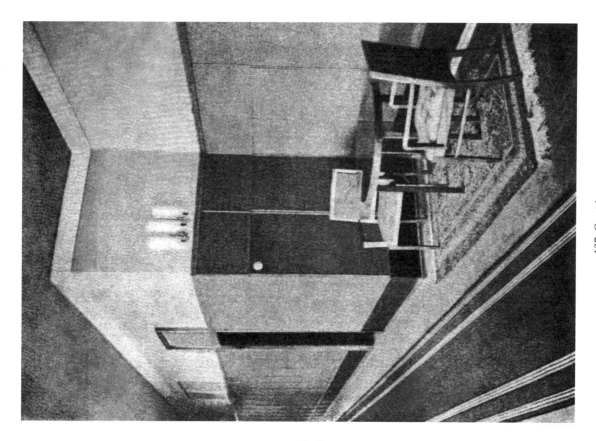

137. Corridor

140. Residential room

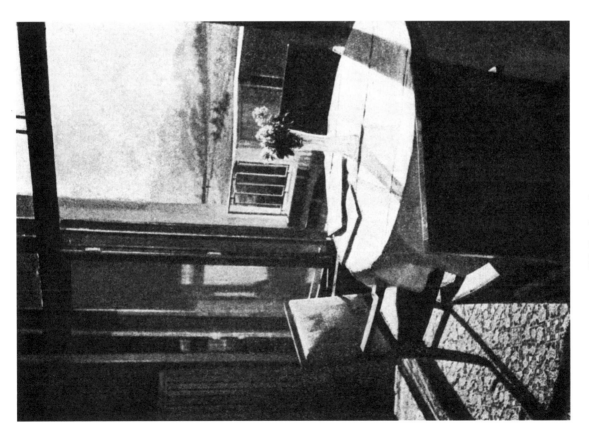

139. Residential room

[83]

141. Roof garden

142. View of the central parterre from the roof

143. View of ancillary structures from the roof of block no. 1

144. General view of ancillary structures

[85]

CONTENTS

This publication is a facsimile reproduction of the Russian-language original, published in 1940 in USSR

Translation by John Nicolson

Editors of English edition: Mark Sutcliffe and Frank Althaus (Fontanka Publications)

© 2019 Ginzburg Design Limited. All rights reserved

Published in 2019 by Ginzburg Design Limited (www.ginzburg-architects.com)
with Fontanka Publications (www.fontanka.co.uk)

All opinions expressed within this publication are those of the authors
and not necessarily of the publishers

British Library Cataloguing-in-Publication Data
A CIP record for this book is available from the British Library

ISBN 978-1-906257-30-9

No part of this publication may be reproduced, stored in a retrieval system,
or transmitted, in any form or by any means, electronic, mechanical, photocopying,
recording, or otherwise, without prior permission of the copyright holder.

Printed in 2019 by SIA "PNB-Print" (Latvia)

ISBN 978-1-906257-30-9

9 781906 257309